# Michigan's Capitol

# Michigan's Capitol

Construction & Restoration

*William Seale*

*Ann Arbor    The University of Michigan Press*
*in association with the Michigan Capitol Committee*

Published in the United States of America by
The University of Michigan Press
Manufactured in the United States of America
Printed on acid-free paper
1998 1997 1996 1995 4 3 2 1

Library of Congress Cataloging-in-Publication Data

Seale, William.
Michigan's Capitol : construction & restoration / William Seale.
p. cm.
ISBN 0-472-09573-0 (alk. paper). — ISBN 0-472-06573-4 (pbk. : alk. paper)
1. Michigan State Capitol (Lansing, Mich.)—Conservation and restoration. 2. Eclecticism in architecture—Michigan—Lansing. 3. Myers, Elijah E., 1832–1909—Criticism and interpretation. 4. Lansing (Mich.)—Buildings, structures, etc. I. Title.
NA4413.L36S43 1994
725´. 11´ 02880977427—dc20 94-38642
CIP

To the Citizens of Michigan:

Michigan history records that, in 1847, Lansing was chosen as the seat of government and " the State Capitol was constructed amid a forest, and another part of the wilderness gave way to civilization." A quarter century later, the cornerstone was laid for this building and, in 1879, Governor Croswell dedicated a new Michigan Capitol.

In the years since, our Capitol stood watch as Michigan put America and the world on wheels. The hard-working men and women of Motown and cities all across Michigan built quality cars that became a part of every family and forever changed the Michigan landscape.

Our Capitol stood watch as Michigan became the "Arsenal of Democracy," building the tanks and the planes that helped America keep the flames of freedom and democracy burning during the dark days of World War II.

Our Capitol stood watch over governors from all walks of life. Farmer Russell Alger, educator Woodbridge Ferris, and war hero and prosecutor Harry Kelly are just a few of the distinctive and dedicated public servants who have governed our state from the hallowed halls of the Capitol.

Our Capitol is the only building in Michigan that stands as a reminder of the accomplishments and the mission of our state government. From 1987 to 1992, a comprehensive restoration transformed a great old building of the past into a powerful symbol of the great things we will achieve in the future.

America's system of democracy is the greatest on earth. Michigan's Capitol celebrates that greatness. The wonderfully restored building is home to the Senate, the House of Representatives, and the Office of the Governor. But more than that, our Capitol is home to an idea—that government belongs to the people.

This is the story of the construction and restoration of our Capitol: please share in Michigan's pride and hope as expressed by its renewal.

Sincerely,

John Engler
*Governor*

# FOREWORD

The Michigan State Capitol stands with great distinction among a group of American statehouses built between the late 1860s and the 1890s. That period, called the Gilded Age, produced buildings which are now recognized as being among the nation's most powerful civic symbols. Michigan's capitol has proven to be of great historical value, and has played a leading role in public art and architecture.

During its first century, the capitol endured neglect and deterioration, as well as many physical changes. Although the capitol continued to function as the seat of state government, these alterations had an adverse effect on the building. Fortunately awareness of the importance of historic buildings in general, and of the Michigan capitol in particular, grew dramatically in the 1970s and 1980s. This awareness and the resulting concern about the eventual fate of the capitol led to its preservation for the future.

The restoration proved to be as fascinating as the building itself. As a result, it was suggested that a book be written to tell the story of this award-winning effort, as well as of the capitol's original construction. In June of 1991, the Honorable John J. H. Schwarz, Chair of the Michigan Capitol Committee, appointed a task force to explore the possibility of publishing such a book.

The task force included Jerry Lawler, Executive Director, Michigan Capitol Committee; Kerry Chartkoff, Capitol Archivist, Michigan Capitol Committee; Willis Snow, Secretary of Senate; Tim Bowlin, Business Director, House of Representatives; Debbie Gearhart, Business Director, House of Representatives; and Nancy Harrison, Director of Operations, Executive Office.

The task force selected William Seale to write the book. An expert on state capitols, he was the interiors and historical consultant for the restoration. Cynthia Ware of Washington, D. C. edited the text; the designer was Jeffry Corbin Design of Traverse City; and the publisher was the University of Michigan Press. Thomas L. Jones, former Executive Director of the Historical Society of Michigan, evaluated the project. Kerry Chartkoff and Jerry Lawler provided resource materials.

Photographers for the project were Gregory Domagalski; Dietrich Floeter; Thomas Gennara Photography; Peter Glendinning; Alan Kamuda; Balthazar Korab; Michael Quillinan; and David A. Trumpie. Historic photographs were supplied by the State Archives of Michigan, the *Lansing State Journal*, and other sources and archives noted in the captions. Their generous assistance is gratefully acknowledged.

The Michigan State Capitol belongs to all the citizens of the state, and it was the goal of the task force to bring this book to as many people as possible. In order to meet this goal without sacrificing quality, additional funding for publication was sought. Support was provided from a variety of sources. The first was a substantial in-kind contribution from the University of Michigan Press. Generous support was also provided by a grant from the W. K. Kellogg Foundation of Battle Creek. Finally, additional contributions were provided by those whose vision, hard work, and expertise helped to make the restoration and renewal of the building a success:

Al and Judith Albright; Architects Four, Inc.; John Canning and Company; The Christman Company; Corbin Design; Robert Darvas and Associates; Data Supplies Company; Erb Lumber (McClelland and Duff); Evergreene Painting Studios, Richard C. Frank, FAIA; General Preservation Corporation; F. D. Hayes Electric Company; Honeywell Corporation; Jefferson Art Lighting; William Johnson and Associates; Johnson Steel Company; Darla Olson; Quinn Evans/Architects; William Reichenbach Company; Schiffer Mason Contractors; William A. Sederburg; Shaw-Winkler, Inc.; Gary Steffy Lighting Design, Inc.; U. S. Axminster; Wigen, Tincknell, Meyer & Associates.

Research for this publication was far-reaching. The assistance of the Library of Michigan and the Bureau of Michigan History, particularly John Curry of the State Archives of Michigan, is deeply appreciated.

Richard C. Frank, FAIA
*State Capitol Preservation Architect*

# CONTENTS

The capitol dome at sunset

*Photo by Thomas Gennara*

# INTRODUCTION

The capitol is best seen at the close of day, when light is slipping away from the stone walls and rising inside the buildings on Michigan Avenue. Then come the shadows and pinkish colors of a summer sunset, or, in winter, the blaze of orange that passes through from the horizon on the west to the tall windows on the east, making them shimmer as if golden lamps had been lighted inside.

Daylight gone, the dome seems to take leave of the rambling structure beneath it and become a phantom bathed in electric light, floating over the town. When it was new, it commanded the air, but now it shares the skyline with tall buildings and airplanes, unknown to mankind a hundred years ago. Still the dome rules the capital city, whether seen from the street or from a plane angling in to make its landing.

The Michigan Capitol represents a powerful idea that led to a good design that was sensibly built. However commendable, that in itself does not make a great building, and the capitol is the premier historic site of the state. It did its job well for nearly a century. When it seemed obsolete, it was repaired and rethought, and, without missing a day of work, was given new life for the century to come. High hopes and good plans do not necessarily insure a great restoration. Yet this is one of the best, not only in its technical and artistic details, but in the strength of the concept that lay behind it.

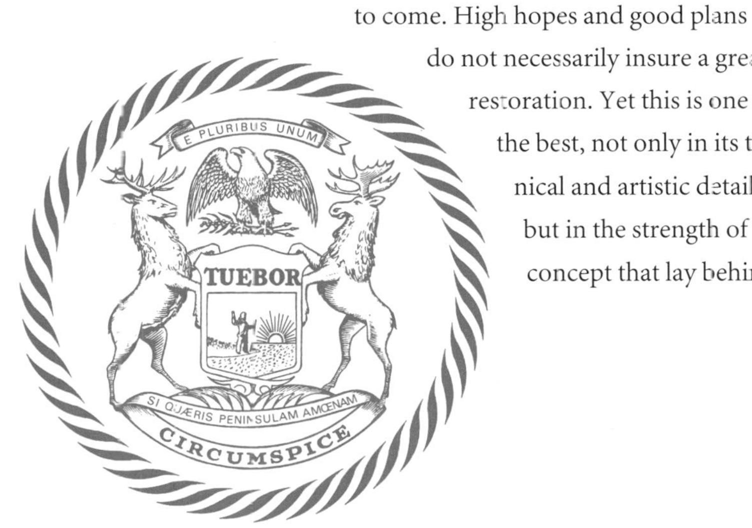

The restored Michigan State Capitol

*Photo by Balthazar Korab*

This book is about the restoration of the Michigan capitol, a joint effort of the legislative and executive branches of the state government carried out from 1987 to 1992. Many heads went together to make the concept of the restoration a reality politically and architecturally. Because there would have been no restoration without a surviving past, the following pages also resurrect the story of the original builders. The decision to restore a building a century old, rather than remodel or replace it, made history more an issue than it might otherwise have been. The restorers studied the early technology and improved and expanded it. They also searched to grasp the original idea that made the building even before the final handshakes on how the work would be done. That idea is its underpinning. That idea the completed restoration praises in its success.

Soldiers of the Fourth Michigan Volunteer Infantry Regiment, mustered in at Adrian. Michigan sent 90,000 such volunteers to the battlefields of the Civil War.

*State Archives of Michigan*

## BACKGROUND

To understand the era that created this flamboyant statehouse, it is necessary to grasp the vast change that came to America and to Michigan with the Civil War. Michigan entered the national limelight. The state's support of the Union cause in the bravery, caring, and sheer number of its fighting men and its universal offering up of good will in the nation's greatest trial inspired a profound sense of nationalism in its citizens that found permanent expression in the new capitol in Lansing. It was begun six years after the close of the war, when some men could still almost smell the gunsmoke of Gettysburg and the earth had hardly settled on the graves in southern soil of thousands who had died.

Matching the emotional fervor generated by the war, technology and invention made an impact on daily life, as the machines of war supply turned in peacetime to domestic markets. Steam powered the railroads that grew by the thousands of miles; steam moved boats along the rivers, the Great Lakes, and the sea; steam revolutionized production in Michigan's salt mines; steam put into action the machines that made carpeting, tin roofing, and other products that were not so commonly available before.

With the flourishing of railroads and the development of towns in southern Michigan, the state, along with the rest of the victorious Union, prospered in the post-Civil War years. By 1870 Michigan led the country in copper mining, and Grand Rapids had challenged the leadership of furniture manufacturing centers in the East. Farms multiplied in the southern part of the state. But most of all it was the booming timber industry that established postwar Michigan's economic prosperity. The vast northern forests covering two-thirds of the Lower Peninsula provided what seemed an endless source of virgin softwood trees—chiefly white pine, but also jack pine and Norway pine—much in demand for building all over the United States. Exploitation of these forests began on a large scale in the late 1860s and continued through the last years of the nineteenth century until the supply was exhausted. Ideas of conservation were still years away. To farmers, who made up the majority of the population, the mass removal of forests was a good thing because it cleared land for crops (although the sandy soil of northern Michigan did not support good farms). Big businesses emerged in the harvesting, processing, and transporting of timber from the northern forests to mills and markets.

Logging on the Saginaw River. Michigan's white pine lumbering era peaked in the 1870s and 1880s. By 1900 most of the pine had been cut.

*State Archives of Michigan*

Michigan's first capitol, in Detroit, served as territorial courthouse until statehood was finally achieved in 1837.

*State Archives of Michigan*

In 1847 the seat of state government moved to Lansing, where a second capitol, intended as temporary, served the state for thirty years.

*State Archives of Michigan*

Lansing had made its debut as capital of Michigan on New Year's Day 1848, when the legislature, having left the old capital of Detroit for a more central location, was called into session. Here was a raw town in a clearing on the banks of the Grand River, climaxed by a prim clapboard statehouse, Greek Revival in style at its pilastered doorway and in the classical conformity of its rectangular shape. The building stood two stories and was crowned by a tin-roofed cupola. In the distance the deep forests of oak, hickory, maple, beech, and ash awaited the axe and plow.

The township fended off challenges to capital status, yet it was obvious that the wooden statehouse was no anchor to keep the government there. The first sounds of the railroad whistle in Lansing early in the war assured convenience of access, but inadequate schedules and poorly maintained tracks made the railroad undependable. Shortcomings of this kind were typical at the time, when so many of those who would have made the state function well were away on southern battlefields. Bad telegraph connections drove parts of the government to Detroit for two years. But during the war ever-increasing numbers of state employees packed Lansing's capitol, threatening the survival of the building and its wood and paper contents with the common dangers of candles, kerosene oil lamps, and sooty woodburning stoves.

When the war was over most of the celebrating took place in Detroit. It was there on July 4, 1866, that the soldiers, back home for good, turned over "123 battered, bullet-torn flags" to Governor Henry Crapo, who put them on display, possibly in the Lansing capitol. These battle flags, relics of valor, remain the most beloved artifacts of the state's past.

The massive July 4, 1866, parade and ceremonies in Detroit in which Michigan celebrated the Union victory and the end of the Civil War

*Burton Historical Collection*

IT MAY HAVE BEEN
THE PRESENCE OF THE FLAGS
THAT SPURRED THE LAWMAKERS
TO ACTION IN BUILDING A
NEW FIREPROOF CAPITOL
TO PROTECT THEM.

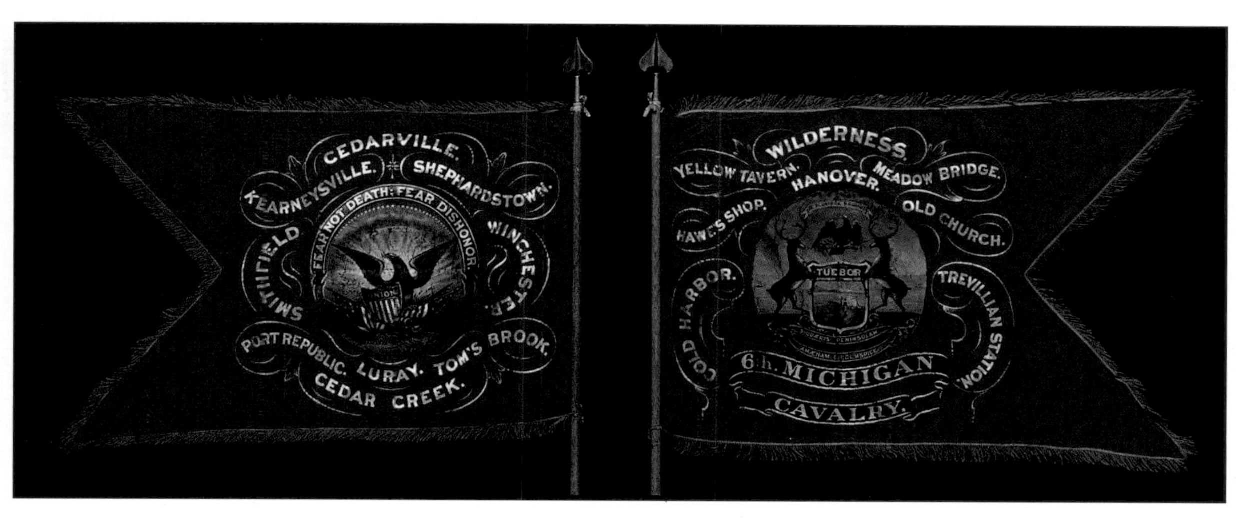


Examples of the brilliant silk regimental battle flags that Michigan volunteers carried throughout the Civil War and defended at great cost. The sight of these flags, according to Michigan Adjutant General John R. Robertson in 1882, "revived in the minds of all recollections of past victories and defeats, of friends lost—and a country saved."

*Photos by Peter Glendinning*

It may have been the presence of the flags that spurred the lawmakers to action in building a new fireproof capitol to protect them. Nine months after the presentation of the flags it was proposed in the House of Representatives that a building and monument be built for the relics. Four years later, on January 4, 1871, Governor Henry P. Baldwin observed in his message to the legislature that "immediate action should be taken to erect a new State House, with capacity sufficient for the proper accommodation of the Legislature and all of the State departments, and commensurate with the present and prospective wants of the State."

The actual bill was introduced in the Senate on February 14, 1871, and passed two weeks later; it passed the House on March 22. The bill called for building in a "leisurely" way, with a statewide tax levy of about twenty cents per person per year until the new capitol was completed.

The legislative events of that spring were great news for Lansing. There was to be a grand and permanent capitol, thus a permanent capital. On the last day of March the governor signed the act of legislature into law as Public Act 67 of 1871, specifying that the total cost of the building, including the architect's fees and all other expenses, not exceed $1.2 million, a sum to be raised by assessing every taxpayer in Michigan 16 7/8 cents per year for six years.

One resident of Lansing, Orien Austin Jenison, was particularly happy. As a young man twenty-four years earlier he had cast his lot with Lansing when it was a wilderness of woods, and now he was to see a great monument take form in its midst, as cathedrals had risen in the ancient towns of Europe. With a sense of history being made, he set himself to create, through clippings, notes, photographs, and souvenirs, a permanent record of the building of the new capitol.

O. A. Jenison

*State Archives of Michigan*

WEST VIRGINIA
SOUTH CAROLINA
FLORIDA

Detail of Elijah Myers's original drawing for the ceiling of the Senate chamber. Such intricate "historical" detail was typical of the taste of the time.

*State Archives of Michigan*

The year 1871 was the third year of the presidency of General Ulysses S. Grant, hero of the triumphant Union. It was the high noon of what Mark Twain called the Gilded Age. For all its apparent excess, his judgment was harsh. If the surface seemed gilt and plaster, nationalism, state pride, and optimism radiated from within, even in official papers and the press. People were eager to do things better than they had been done in the past. It was the Gilded Age impulse to build grandly that made Michigan's capitol a reality. The time was right. Two years later, with the nation swamped in a national depression—the Panic of 1873—prudent officials would probably have shrunk from such an endeavor.

During this time Michigan's governors, like most of its residents, were not natives. Governor Baldwin, who proposed the new capitol, was a Rhode Islander who had moved to Michigan while a young man to establish a shoe business, then made his fortune in banking. His successor in 1873, John J. Bagley, had moved to Michigan from New York State as a boy and by the age of 21 owned a chewing tobacco factory, the basis of his fortune. Governor Charles M. Croswell, who was to dedicate the capitol in 1879, had also came from New York State while very young and had grown to be one of Michigan's leading legal minds.

In April Governor Baldwin named the Board of State Building Commissioners who were to guide the work. He included himself as president and ex officio member, with three appointed members: Ebenezer O. Grosvenor, a Jonesville banker; James Shearer, a Bay City businessman familiar with architectural drawings and building contracts; and Alexander Chapoton, a contractor in Detroit. By the close of day on April 11, it had all been done: the commissioners had filed their bonds and taken oaths not to be party to any contracts for the project. The new capitol was, in a sense, under way.

To prepare themselves, the commissioners voted in May to make an "observation tour" by train to Illinois, Wisconsin, and New York, all of which had new capitols. It was a strange selection. Neither the New York capitol in Albany nor the Illinois capitol in Springfield was complete, and the one in Madison,

Governor Henry P. Baldwin

Ebenezer O. Grosvenor

James Shearer

Alexander Chapoton

*All: State Archives of Michigan*

The New York capitol in Albany under construction, as the Michigan Board of State Building Commissioners might have seen it in 1871

*New York State Capitol Symposium*

Wisconsin, was an odd, castle-like confection from antebellum days. The controversial capitol in Albany, proposed just before the close of the Civil War, had been designed as a towered pile, but like the new capitol in Springfield, which was to have a dome, it stood unfinished. The most that could be learned about either of these was from architects' drawings, although the existing walls showed that they were to be buildings of great scale. The Wisconsin capitol, very much smaller than the other two, was complete. An alteration in its design, however, illustrated a new turn in the long course of capitol architecture.

Since the early nineteenth century American capitol architecture had adopted certain architectural ideas that found expression in columned porticoes, central rotundas, balanced wings expressing bicameral legislatures, and domes. The last element, the dome, had a varied career. In its origin, the feature was not a dome, but a tower, introduced in the Pennsylvania statehouse in Philadelphia—later Independence Hall—in colonial times. The idea of an exterior vertical element to denote a government building took varying forms, mostly lanterns or cupolas such as that built on the old wooden capitol in Lansing, because, in the early years of the country, most capitols or statehouses were no more monumental than that simple structure.

When the Maryland statehouse in Annapolis was remodeled in the 1780s to lure Congress to move the federal government there, a dome was added to heighten the monumentality of the brick structure. The dome was the central feature of the national Capitol in Washington, completed in the 1820s, and had its day in state capitols until the late 1830s, when, in the most ambitious of the new monumental capitols, the dome began to die out in a return to the lantern and tower, now built on grand scale, as in Columbus, Ohio, and Nashville, Tennessee.

New York's decision to incorporate towers in the Albany capitol, which the Michigan commissioners saw only as foundations and walls, was a predictable following of the trend. As the designs of all public building types are in one way or another marked by history, and capitol buildings preeminently so, the Civil War intervened in the ascendancy of capitol towers. In Washington the national Capitol had been expanded through the 1850s to include large wings to the north and south and a great new dome of iron. At the first cannons of war, work was stopped on the dome and soldiers occupied the unfinished Capitol.

The Wisconsin capitol in Madison, as it appeared to the commissioners in 1871

*State Historical Society of Wisconsin*

Winning entry in the 1867 Illinois capitol competition. In 1871, construction on the new capitol, located in Springfield, was just underway.

*Illinois State Historical Library*

The United States Capitol in an 1846 photograph (top); a post–Civil War engraving showing the Capitol with east and west extensions and a larger and much more monumental dome (bottom).

*Top: Architect of the Capitol*
*Bottom: Collection Jerry Lawler*

## COMPROMISE, IF UNNATURAL TO ART, IS THE WAY OF POLITICS.

President Lincoln ordered the troops out and construction to resume as a sign to the people that the Union would continue. In the war's dark first years the many thousands who entered Washington were confronted with the dome. On its completion it became the symbol of Union, an image against the sky cherished by the generation that won the war.

It was in the otherwise archaic capitol in Madison in 1871 that the dome was dramatized as a capitol element for the visitors from Michigan. The new building had been occupied just before the Civil War, but construction had been stopped because of the war, omitting for the time the Moorish-style dome that was to complete the exotic motif. After the war construction was resumed, but the dome as originally designed was scrapped in favor of a new one modeled on that in Washington. The drawings of the capitol in Springfield boasted a similar monumental dome. There would never be one in Albany, for the idea could never be reconciled with the Gothic structure. New York's commissioners were not inclined to reconsider, even when their counterparts in Connecticut decided on a dome in place of the tower proposed for the new Gothic-style capitol. Compromise, if unnatural to art, is the way of politics. New York's capitol was never really finished. The work dragged on in hot controversy for thirty years, with the final solution a building magnificent in some parts, but on the whole too complex and even confused in its image to be a successful public building, much less a capitol.

Back home, the Michigan commissioners appointed Allen L. Bours as secretary and agreed to pay him $1,200 per year to serve as their liaison and carry out their wishes. A burly man whose strident manner fit his appearance, Bours was a bookkeeper in the state treasurer's office. He seemed just the person necessary to manage the office side of the capitol work, although as it turned out he would meddle at other levels. The commissioners seem to have made a wise choice. Although he was considered something of a bully and was feared by subordinates, Bours was devoted to his job. Through good times and bad, even during his own trial for assault and battery, he would be instrumental in the progress of the capitol, from its planning to its completion. When Bours began work in June, the process began in earnest. On the fifth of that month the board phrased an advertisement for an architect to submit designs and plans. It was to be published in newspapers in Lansing, Detroit, Chicago, and New York, with competition entries due five months later, on the first of December.

Allen L. Bours

*State Archives of Michigan*

The advertisement left architectural style to the applicant but was very specific about technical requirements. Michigan's capitol was to be 742 feet east to west and 660 feet north to south, a vast structure indeed, with three and perhaps four floors. It was to have steam heat, gas lighting, and good ventilation. The advertisement stated a budget of $1 million, which, the commissioners

Built in 1854 on land set aside for a permanent capitol, Michigan's first state office building was enlarged in 1863. This handsome Italianate structure was razed in 1871 to make room for the new capitol after a temporary replacement was built on another site.

*State Archives of Michigan*

believed, would insure a good design "avoiding extreme and superfluous ornaments." Drawings submitted were to include exterior elevations for the four facades and specified sections through the building, all at a scale of one-eighth inch to one foot.

In addition the applicant was to provide a full schedule of materials. The requirement of specifications this detailed for a building project was relatively recent and was still by no means common. Traditionally the architect had supplied the builder with as many drawings as they agreed adequately described the proposed building, and if there were any specifications at all, they were mainly simple, descriptive ones: less specifications as we understand the word than directions. The builder himself worked out the details of execution.

The old process, which had worked well, remained the rule with most houses and commercial buildings. Its demise elsewhere came as a result of various forces. With the growth of manufacturing technology, the creative role of the builder eroded away in an avalanche of factory-produced architectural parts that were brought to the site to be combined in one element or another, for example, an iron structural system or a furnace. These were specified by the architect, not designed by either him or the builder. Most monumental projects were public, and the bidding system, always more or less in force, became more highly developed, the architect providing not only the design but a rather specific plan for how to build. Even at their most detailed, specifications then did not compare with those demanded today; but officials believed that this information gave them a safer idea of cost and protected them from pitfalls. The financial success of the Michigan Capitol project would seem to prove the theory.

The advertisement went out to the press on schedule. O. A. Jenison duly pasted a copy in his scrapbook number one. Prizes were offered, $2,000 for first place, $1,000 for second, and $500 for third. It was not said, but implied, that by making these awards the commissioners could borrow and combine from among the three. The summer of 1871 was hot and dry. In Lansing Allen Bours was occupied with the construction of a temporary office building on the square where the old statehouse stood. It cost $30,693.94, exceeding the appropriation by only $693.94 for the addition of a "burglar proof" lining to the vault in the state treasurer's office. The commissioners congratulated themselves.

The parched summer drifted into a rainless autumn unusual for that part of the world. Then on October 8 fire broke out in the lumber district on the west side of Chicago and, fanned by wild storm winds, spread over two miles in the first six hours. At about the same time forests in Michigan began to burn. It was widely believed that sparks carried from Chicago over Lake Michigan by the wind caused the weeks of destruction and chaos that followed. Losses in timber extended into the millions. The capitol commission office in Lansing began to receive letters from the Chicago competitors asking for a postponement of the upcoming December deadline because their competition drawings had been lost in the fire.

A four-week delay ended on December 28, 1871. Although there had been at least eighty inquiries, Bours logged in only twenty sets of drawings on the deadline day. From one of these the new capitol would be built. After deliberations of just under one month, first place was awarded to Elijah E. Myers, an architect with a practice in Springfield, Illinois.

His scheme was for a broad, decorative structure of stone in the Renaissance mode, surmounted by a tall, slender dome of iron, with a style all its own, but enough reflection of the glorious dome in Washington to carry the hour.

On Thursday morning, July 25, 1872, laborers ...broke the ground unceremoniously on Capitol Square.

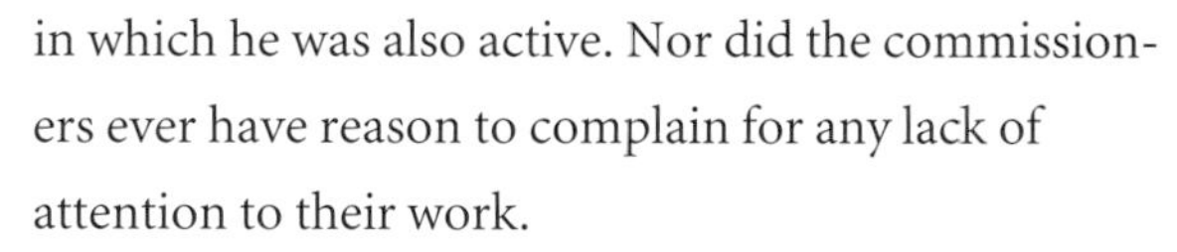

At the time the winning candidate was announced, the commissioners declared their intention to ask the legislature to proceed with the entire $1.2 million appropriation, rather than making it in parts. So complete did they feel their plan was, with its specifications, that they requested permission to engage a single contractor and pursue the work for an uninterrupted six years. The legislature approved. Advertisements for contractors in May brought six proposals on July 11, only one of which was from Michigan (H. Richards, from Jackson). Two were from New York and two from Illinois, and one was from Pennsylvania. The highest bid was $1,891,000 from I. L. Loomis and George S. Hebard of Illinois, and low bidder was Nehemiah Osburn & Co., of Rochester, New York, at $1,208,000. The commissioners went to the table with Osburn and pulled the price down to the appropriated figure. Osburn then had the job.

Nehemiah Osburn

*Rochester Historical Society*
*Rochester, New York*

Osburn, a native of Pompey, New York, was a well-established contractor in Rochester, a rich man who occupied an elegant, snowy white Greek Revival mansion on East Avenue, Rochester's finest residential street. Seventy years old in 1871, he had been in the building business for fifty years, more if one considers his boyhood training as a carpenter. The growth of his company had come from federal, state, and county government contracts. He built custom houses in Chicago and Milwaukee and the United States Courthouse in Baltimore. Like Elijah Myers, Osburn had learned the advantages the railroads gave a company, making it possible to be here today and there tomorrow, building a small-city contracting firm into a business that could call itself national. Never while he worked on the Michigan capitol would Osburn waver in his strict schedule of moving between Rochester and Lansing. In spite of his years, he kept many pots going at the same time, both in building projects and in banking, in which he was also active. Nor did the commissioners ever have reason to complain for any lack of attention to their work.

O. A. Jenison clipped the July 11 *Lansing State Republican,* which announced the results of the bidding and said that work would begin on the site within several days. "Since the adoption of the design by the Commissioners there has been a large increase in the cost of building materials, especially iron and plate glass, which represent fully one-third of the cost of the building, and it was feared by many that the work must consequently be abandoned until a further appropriation could be obtained, or that a less costly building should be constructed. It is the intention of the Commissioners to confine themselves strictly to the act, and they expect to give the people as good a building for $1,200,000.00 as other States have paid double that amount for."

On Thursday morning, July 25, 1872, laborers working under Osburn's foreman, Charles W. Butler, broke the ground unceremoniously on Capitol Square. By the specifications they were to excavate "two feet larger than required by the entire area of the plans, and five feet deep below the ground-line." The instructions continued, "Dig the trenches for all outside foundation walls three feet deep below the said line of excavation, and for inside foundation walls, two feet below said line. Make the bottom of trenches perfectly level, and sides plumb... Do all digging required to build sewers, air-ducts, cess-pools, areas, and foundations for all steps, and for the engine and fuel rooms. The spaces between the bank and exterior walls must be filled in with earth; thoroughly rammed with wooden rammers and brought up to the proper level on the line of building." With these simple instructions, written in ink in Secretary Bours's flowery hand, the Michigan capitol was begun.

An oil painting created by Joseph F. DuMont for the Elijah Myers Room in the capitol depicts Myers as a young architect in Springfield. Drawings on his drafting table show his entries in the Michigan capitol competition.
*Photo by Custom Photographic, Lansing*

Elijah E. Myers, architect, had captured a star for his crown. By 1872 he was a long way from home. Little is known about him until this time, when, with the Michigan capitol, he began a near-thirty-year career as a prolific architect and builder of public buildings, notably state capitols. The history of his earlier life, put together from small pieces, remains dim. Yet it helps form a picture. The earliest known about him dates from 1860, when he was already a grown man, a carpenter living in the Frankford district of Philadelphia among other tradesmen and many foreign tongues. From the style of his letters it is assumed that he was American-born.

He had some connection with the famous Philadelphia architect Samuel Sloan, perhaps first as a carpenter and later as an architect. One of the leading architects of his day, Sloan deserves some attention in connection with Myers. He listed himself in Philadelphia's city directories in two ways, as "carpenter," which he had been since his youth, and as "architect," a more recent and at that time less stable designation. The quality of his designs and his acclaimed publications on houses and public buildings made him famous in his field, though something of a renegade compared to his more illustrious Philadelphia contemporary, Thomas U. Walter, architect of the great dome on the Capitol in Washington and also a veteran of the building trades. Sloan's work was spread far and wide through the United States in the 1850s, 1860s, and 1870s. Hardly a major project existed that did not involve him in some way, if only in an application to do the work. His projects ranged from courthouses to schools to private residences. In 1853 he designed the State Hospital in Kalamazoo, Michigan, now demolished, and while it was being built, he commenced the celebrated octagon mansion, Longwood, near Natchez, Mississippi, which still stands unfinished beneath its onion dome, abandoned by Sloan's Philadelphia workmen at the first cannon fire of the Civil War. Sloan closed his office in 1862 for the duration of the war, but quickly cashed in on the postwar building boom. While Myers was making his bid to design the Michigan capitol, Sloan reaped a major contract to remodel and expand the capitol of New Jersey.

No document thus far has linked Myers absolutely to Sloan's buildings, either as a workman or a draftsman, but few records of Sloan's office are extant. The man through whom we know Sloan best, Addison Hutton, an employee and later partner, never mentions Myers in his papers. It is known that Myers used Sloan freely as a reference, so it seems reasonable to assume that he worked for or with him at some point. Myers's own aggressiveness as a businessman would suggest Sloan as his model, as well. And while it may have been coincidence, Myers moved from Philadelphia to Springfield, Illinois, the year after Sloan closed his practice. Myers is said to have been in the wartime Army Corps of Engineers, but his name is not among the documents of the corps.

In Springfield, now styling himself "architect," he watched the Illinois capitol competition of 1867, which signaled the coming of a series of grand prairie capitols. Because he imitated certain features of this building, it must have impressed him. Doubtless he knew the winners, a builder-turned-architect named J. C. Cochrane, of Chicago, and his employee Alfred H. Piquenard, an engineer trained in his native France. He was their competitor in 1871 in Lansing. When he won the Michigan competition, Myers moved his wife and two children to Detroit, where he would live for the rest of his life, beginning a career like Sloan's, which took him everywhere in pursuit of great public works.

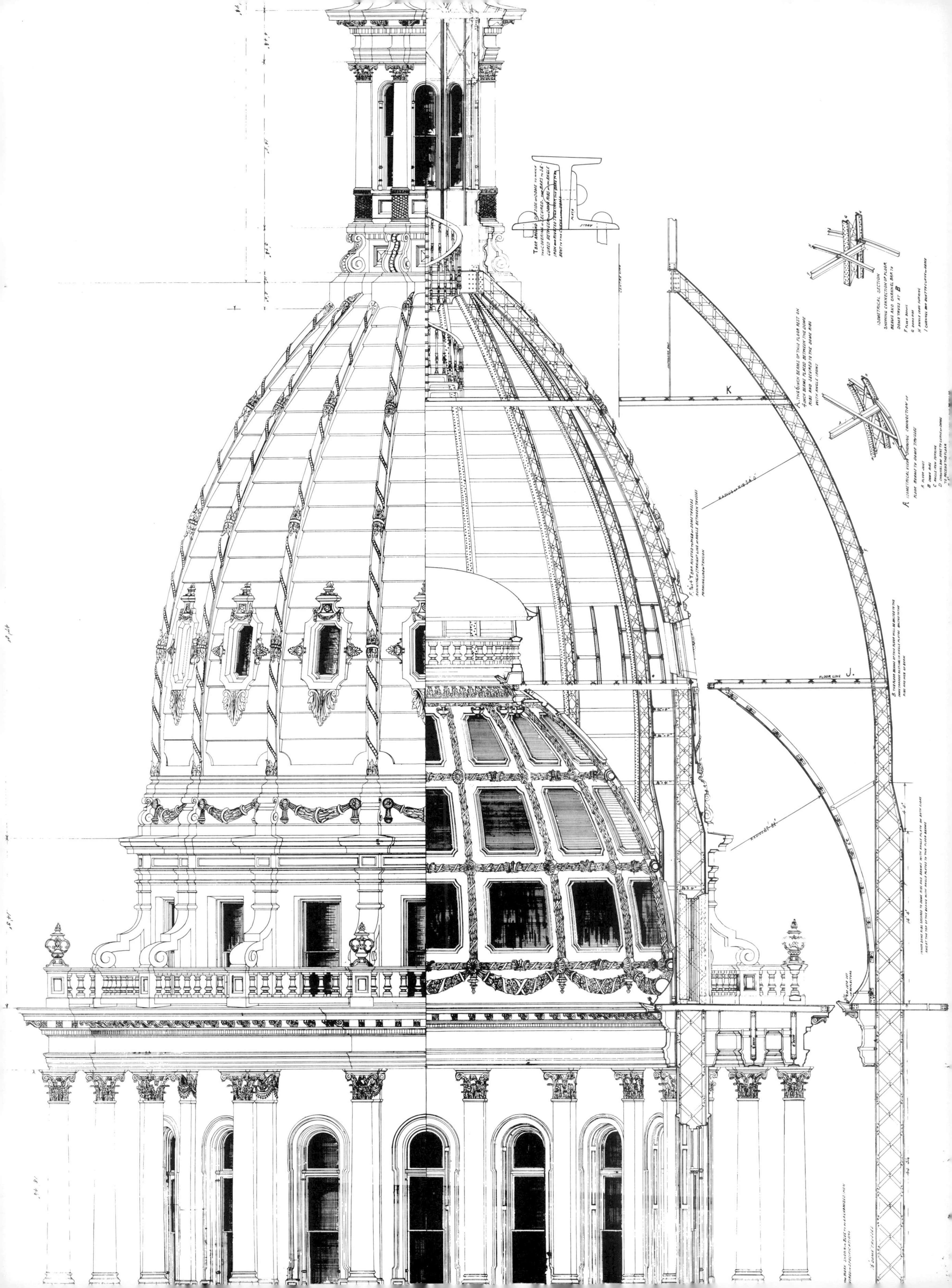

Detail of Myers's drawing of the iron dome shows the outer skin, the inner dome, and the iron ribs which support the structure.

*State Archives of Michigan*

The drawings that won Michigan's 1871 capitol design competition still survive. That they were drawn by Myers himself seems confirmed by their close resemblance to all the drawings associated with his other projects. They show the building much as built. Penned on oiled linen sheets nearly a yard square, they are all in ink, with occasional pencil corrections or adjustments. After fixing the linen page to his drawing board with string, Myers would have drawn first lightly in pencil, then in ink, which he mixed himself from powder. There were no erasures except for a quick wipe-away almost as soon as a mark had been made, so Myers's skill as a draftsman is proven in the intricacies of his technique. His lines are firmly laid, his shading effective, in fine parallel lines, close together. The drawings show a flair for the flamboyant in their acanthus leaves and scrolls, as does the resulting building.

Cartouche from a drawing by Myers

Taken as a whole, the drawings and the accompanying specifications are by today's laden standards very terse. In the old manner, they give the idea. As to details of construction, the contractor still had much to say. Myers was also conversant with the building trades; he and the builder could communicate. Old ways thus remained along with the new. Members of the trades were all wage earners, no longer paid by the job. Many classifications of tradesmen would work in frequent council with Myers and Osburn. (Time would see many of these trades vanish. The idea would come to prevail that a building can be built first entirely on paper. But that was thirty years away.)

The building Myers proposed for Michigan was smaller than the commissioners had specified. No reason can be found for the reduction to about half the proposed size, although the commission must have ordered it. Myers's plan measured 336 feet end to end and 180 feet at its deepest part, through the center. It would in fact be a little larger. The "grand dome" that was to crown it all would reach high above anything then standing in Michigan. The building itself, a broad horizontal structure with central block, wings, and embellishments of pilasters and carvings in stone, showed the influence of the expanded Capitol in Washington. Although Myers's design had suggested Lincoln's large, columned dome, it was not the same. Myers composed his scheme in modern iron frame and cast-iron plates, like that built in Washington, but took inspiration for its design from the dome of the early eighteenth-century church central to France's largest military hospital complex, the Hôtel des Invalides in Paris. The Invalides dome was famous less as architecture than as the splendid canopy over the tomb of Napoleon.

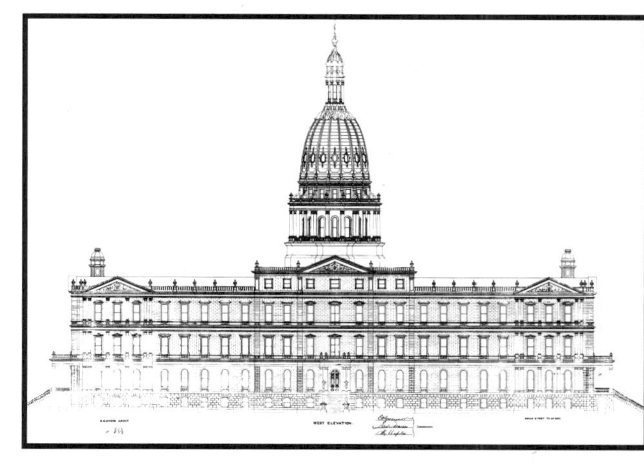

An early drawing of the capitol's west elevation, as submitted by Elijah Myers and approved by the Board of State Building Commissioners

*State Archives of Michigan*

To review the drawings...
is to have that exuberance
of 1871 revived.

Myers's interest extended far beyond the architecture of the new capitol. Here are his front, side, and perspective views of a chair to be used by the presiding officer in the House and Senate chambers. The chairs were built and survive today.

*State Archives of Michigan*

Myers did not have to know the French model at all, for Cochrane and Piquenard had already used the Invalides dome in Springfield and Des Moines. The version for Michigan was different, however; as with most of Myers's architectural work, here was his own erratic touch, in this case an elongation of the element into a vertical, bottle-like form that in a sense very slightly challenged the necessary perception that it derived from the great bulbous dome in Washington.

Apart from the dome, the capitol was not so literal in its translation of historical sources, although it clearly represents an effort to be historical. Today it is most readily labeled Renaissance Revival. Myers called it "Palladian," but the name has no more meaning here than when it was used by Cochrane and Piquenard of their entry in the nearly contemporary capitol competition in Des Moines. Myers's Michigan capitol is quite different from its monumental contemporaries in the restraint of its ornament and its total departure from the French, or Second Empire, flavoring prevalent in American public architecture at the time. Both the drawings and the completed building—and they were one and the same—bear a resemblance to old City Hall in New York, an early nineteenth-century neoclassical structure designed by Joseph François Mangin and John McComb, Jr. The massing is virtually the same, with a central block a full story higher than the rest, decorated with stone pilasters, and two heavy wings similarly adorned, each connected to the main section by relatively simple, smooth-walled wings of a narrower dimension.

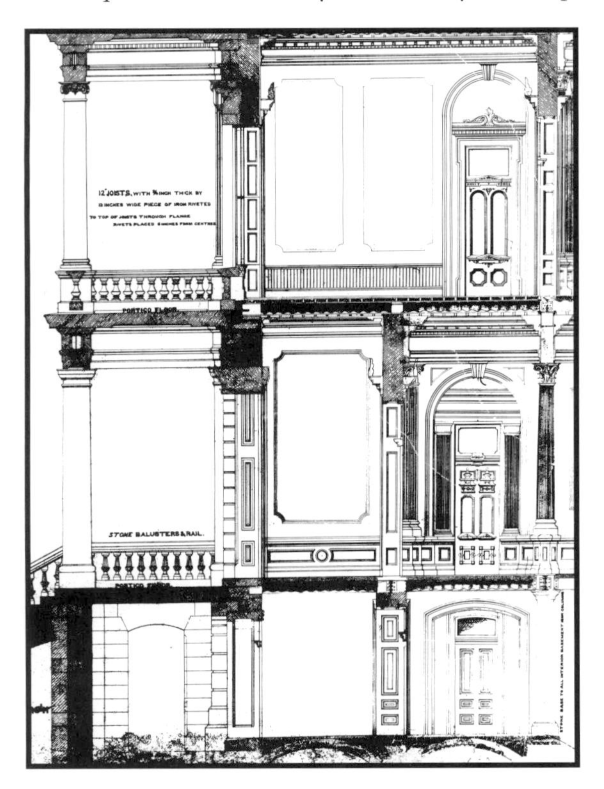


Detail of a cross section of the capitol. Successive floors feature differing corridor treatments, adding richness to the design.

*State Archives of Michigan*

It would have been odd for an architect in 1871 to so boldly adopt the American "colonial"—meaning at the time merely "antique"—for a modern public building, for the Colonial Revival was as yet a few years away, and, in the sense of literal imitation, some years to come. America's most recognized and praised architects turned to Europe for their ideas, as with the Second Empire forms in Des Moines and Springfield. One might, however, find this sort of adventurousness in Myers, who had remained somewhat detached from the developing professional field of architecture and was less likely to consider himself part of a design movement. He might take his models where he chose. Like Sloan, he had come to the field not through formal training in architecture, but through the building trades. He was building a capitol. What worked, worked; and the historical reference in this building, which is difficult to deny, provides one of its few subtleties, in an age more easily pleased by bolder strokes.

Perhaps Myers's familiarity with Philadelphia played some part, for history was much in the air there as the city prepared to celebrate with a world's fair the 100th anniversary of the Declaration of Independence. City Hall in Manhattan was considered by those interested in building one of the finest structures ever erected in the United States (and it holds that honor with ease still today). Such an architectural motif might even have been useful to Myers in selling his idea in Michigan, where a significant portion of the population had migrated earlier in the century from New York State. So far as is known Myers never wrote a line to confirm the connection, but no sources discount the idea, either.

Details of capitol doors. On the left is the design of the "hall side" doors; on the right, the interior office doors.

*State Archives of Michigan*

The original drawings, housed today in the State Archives of Michigan, show detail as detail was known in 1871. Myers designed all the interior woodwork, the marble floors, and the cast-iron stairs, columns, and other iron elements, which were ultimately custom made in Philadelphia. He designed some cabinetry and furniture, showing a bold taste for the heavy, carved Renaissance Revival and the more subtle *néo-grec,* both the most modern of ideas at the time. It is almost certain that he designed the voluptuous gas lighting fixtures of the corridors and rostrums, although drawings do not exist. His touch of splendor and decoration flowed over every plane and crevice like a frothy liquid. His capitol was to be a native sort of creation, a palatial vision to take root in the existing man-made landscape of small wooden houses, where it would seem magnificent beyond most people's grandest dreams.

To review the drawings, now somewhat darkened from nearly a century and a quarter of life, is to have that exuberance of 1871 revived. The plans show spaces so huge and numerous that Myers struggled to find purposes for all of them. One series of rooms was designated as a residence for the lieutenant governor, and though the idea does not appear anywhere else in this capitol's history, such a suite is still in use in the capitol Myers was later to design for Texas. The Michigan planners were building more than they needed, but what about the next years and decades? Time would see the rooms filled (and how true this was to be). Myers drew his scheme as though he were designing a palace. Page after page of sometimes intricate, often extravagant drawings for columns and pediments delight the eye and sometimes amuse with their innocent interpretations of the western world's architectural past. But history was only a thin veneer. There are many more drawings for steam boilers, fireproof ceilings, brick arching, and the mighty bones of bolted iron that gave the building its structure, to remind us that Myers's was an age of racing technology in which what was best was not past, but present.

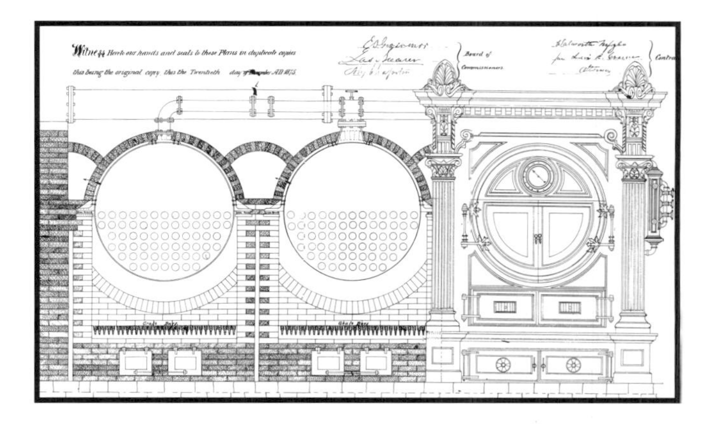

Myers's elevation drawing of the great boilers of the capitol's steam heating system

*State Archives of Michigan*

BOOTS AND SHOES
A. ABER
BOOTS & SHOES.
BOOTS
DETROIT ALE

Ceremony for the laying of the cornerstone for the new capitol, October 2, 1873. Over thirty thousand enthusiastic spectators crowded into Lansing from all over the state to witness the festive event, the largest crowd to gather in the capital city for many years.
*State Archives of Michigan*

# CONSTRUCTION

Nehemiah Osburn assembled materials at the site, as the workmen dug out the basement through yellowish clay and varying strata. In August 1872 he reported progress on the excavation, which was completed in September, its size the wonder of all who saw it. Then came the foundation of poured concrete, made from a base of pulverized limestone. A special steam crusher was hauled to the site. Meanwhile a carpenters' shop was under construction. There were also a blacksmith shop and a lime house for working up lime into plaster and mortar. Twenty thousand tons of sandstone arrived for the first courses of the walls. Brick came from the brickyard of George B. Hall. A man only in his twenties, Hall bid on the work and established his yard outside Lansing upon receiving the contract. Business boomed, and other contracts followed. In the spring of 1873 he was employing some sixty men and women, and made special note of the efficiency of women at the craft. The inner structure of the capitol would be of brick, which would back the outer stone walls. Brick made of clay from a depth of four feet "burned cherry red" in the kiln, while deeper clay produced a white or cream color. Both would be used in the walls and arches of the capitol.

Brick walls uncovered during the restoration of the capitol. Fifteen million locally produced bricks were used to build its walls and floors.
*Michigan Capitol Committee*

Excavation for the capitol foundation began in July 1872. Approximately 17,000 cubic yards of earth were removed before the excavation was completed in December 1872. Derricks used to lift huge blocks of stone for the outer walls can be seen in the foreground.
*State Archives of Michigan*

"THERE WERE NO HOUSES TO BE HAD BY THE VERITABLE ARMY OF STONE CUTTERS, BRICKLAYERS, MASONS AND CARPENTERS THAT SWARMED IN HERE FOR THE BUILDING OF THE CAPITOL."

Myers, given superintendence of the entire project, commuted frequently from Detroit. He set up his headquarters with Allen Bours in the commissioners' office when it moved from the old capitol into a new wooden structure of two stories built to the left of the east gate to the fenced capitol grounds. Oliver Marble was employed as his assistant superintendent. Already Myers had prepared a view of the new capitol, which he hung on his wall. An engraving was made of this to be sold. A newspaper correspondent from Detroit found the office "filled with plans for the new structure." Indeed, "his subordinates are around him busily celebrating other designs which he has in charge." Everywhere were samples: bricks, tiles, stone. One could take two of Mr. Hall's excellent bricks, smack them together, and hear an almost metallic sound. And the stone decided on was from Amherst, Ohio. Samples of it could be seen by anyone who cared to call at the architect's office.

The builders began to assemble. Many were foreign-born, and as almost a mirror of the building trades in America at the time, most seem to have been Scottish, Irish, German, or Dutch. In 1872 a master stonemason, Eban McPhee, moved to Lansing. His story was probably typical. He had left hard times in Scotland to find better work in New York. The great fire had attracted him to Chicago, where he made a reputation that caught the eye of Richard Glaister, head of stonecutting for the capitol, who offered him better wages than he could make in Chicago. Johanna McPhee, his wife, remembered many years later the situation in Lansing when she and McPhee arrived: "There were no houses to be had by the veritable army of stone cutters, bricklayers, masons and carpenters that swarmed in here for the building of the Capitol." Even with the promise of good money, all the McPhees could secure for shelter were rooms over a store.

The numbers of workmen varied from time to time during construction. Many, like McPhee, left Chicago's lively building market to try their luck with the Michigan capitol. No convict labor seems to have been used, which was unusual for a capitol project. Workers who moved to Lansing in the late summer and through the fall of 1872 found themselves trapped by the terrible winter of that year. Foundation concrete that had set was packed in earth and straw against the weather, and most of the men were without work from mid-November to mid-April 1873. They were, in our terminology, laid off, with a skeleton crew retained at short hours. This can only have been devastating to most, but it was typical of building projects of the time.

As the winds and snows swept through in succession, the legislators appeared more concerned over the cornerstone ceremony than the winter standstill. Governor Baldwin, though thwarted by the weather, had wanted the foundations completed by the end of his term, New Year's Day. Barring that, he wanted the cornerstone laid. He got neither, although the legislature, responding to a general enthusiasm about the capitol, decided that the cornerstone ceremony must be scheduled. But the date had not been set by January, when Governor John J. Bagley took office.

The stonemasons' lodge on the capitol construction site. Stacked in the foreground is some of the almost 700,000 cubic feet of stone used in construction.

*State Archives of Michigan*

No decision was reached until April 24, 1873, when the ceremony was scheduled for September.

Work was again under way. Spirits had improved, and with the cornerstone deadline, the project moved along at a fast pace. Allen Bours had journeyed to Albany, New York, during the winter to inspect and evaluate close at hand the way in which the state administered the great though ill-starred capitol project going on there. What he learned helped him formulate administrative procedures for Lansing, although he found New York accounting practices too loose for Michigan. Closely supervised by the commissioners, he was a stickler for careful records. His job was to keep the office on even keel and the work within budget.

The person most closely associated with actual construction was James Appleyard, a skilled construction superintendent who had worked for Osburn in Rochester since before the Civil War. An Englishman by birth and the son of a master builder who emigrated to central New York, Appleyard was the manager for Osburn on site. He had served the company on several major projects, including work done for the Supervising Architect of the U.S. Treasury in building post offices in Chicago, Baltimore, and Milwaukee. No construction project can proceed well without an Appleyard, and he had long since proved his worth to Osburn. It was his job to coordinate the work of the subcontractors and direct construction. As Osburn's employee, he reported directly to his company, but in practice he interacted with the commissioners and Bours, and so much with the community that he settled in Lansing and lived there the rest of his life. He worked well with Myers and would build Detroit's city hall for him later on.

Myers himself performed well on this capitol project. In years to come, in his work on courthouses, capitols, and other public buildings, he would be accused of laxity, of taking on too much other work to leave proper time for the business at hand. This was not so in Lansing, even though Myers was busily applying for projects elsewhere, mostly courthouses, and had others on his drawing board. One wonders if the good management provided by Osburn and the commissioners was the reason the work went so smoothly in this instance.

James Appleyard

*State Archives of Michigan*

DERRICKS FOR MOVING HEAVY STONE STOOD UP FROM THE PLANE OF THE REST LIKE PREHISTORIC BEASTS, DIPPING, RAISING, AND SWAYING THEIR BURDENS FROM ONE SPOT TO ANOTHER.

The site was filled with people, activity, and raw pine buildings that served the various trades. In addition to the carpenters' shop a stonemasons' lodge had been built, a long, open-sided shed with heavy workbenches along the sides and down the center. The first singing of chisels had emanated from there in October 1872. Railroad tracks had been extended near enough to the site so that the Amherst sandstone, having been transported by rail the 200 miles from its Ohio quarry, could be unloaded on a convenient holding platform adjacent to the river bridge on Michigan Avenue and drawn a mere two blocks down the street to the capitol. Horses and mules did the everyday hauling of dirt, rubble, tools, and lumber. Roads crisscrossed the square haphazardly, defining the shortest routes both to Michigan Avenue and other streets around the site and to various work places. Derricks for moving heavy stone stood up from the plane of the rest like prehistoric beasts, dipping, raising, and swaying their burdens from one spot to another.

Central to the scene was the great hole. Citizens walking around the fence after working hours could get a sense of the magnitude of the capitol from its footprint. If foundations usually seem smaller than the building they will support, the contrary seems to have been true of the capitol, which was described with awe by those who saw it at this stage. In June 1873 more than a hundred men were at work at the site, concentrating on the foundation.

Preparations for the autumn cornerstone laying surely rivaled in attention, conference, and newspaper comment arrangements the British make for coronations. The commission met frequently, deliberating over such details as music and decoration. This project was a big event for Lansing. It was time to crow, and the mayor and city officials took an active part in the event. In June the polished granite cornerstone was ordered from Struthers & Sons granite works in Philadelphia, at a cost of $400. The inscription "A.D. 1872" was ordered for the east face, while on the north side a prudent "A.D. 187–" awaited insertion of the completion date. All manner of complications beset this committee, as they will most such committees, not the least being the conflict of the appointed cornerstone day with many county fairs in Michigan. This was to be a statewide celebration.

The capitol's five-ton cornerstone, of granite quarried in Massachusetts, sits near the speaker's stand, waiting for the start of the dedication ceremonies.

*State Archives of Michigan*

At the cornerstone ceremony on Capitol Square, flags floated from derricks garlanded with evergreens, and Civil War battle flags decorated the speaker's stand.

*State Archives of Michigan*

By August the *State Republican* could note the first accident among the workmen. James Moore was operating a crane when the crank slipped out of the cogs and flew against his face, breaking his nose "in a frightful manner." Johanna Appleyard, wife of James Appleyard, died of a heart condition soon after. "She was a native of Ireland, and a Catholic in faith," went the announcement in the local newspaper. "Her genial ways and charitable heart had won many friends, who now sorrow with the grief-stricken husband." The capitol project was shut down for three days of mourning. (A year later, almost to the day, Appleyard married Augusta Sanborn of Appleton, Wisconsin.)

The first stones were set on the concrete foundation at the southeast corner of the building in June. These "footing stones" would form a submerged wall four feet high, upon which the actual exposed stone base of the building would stand. By late August the outline of the building was about half defined in stone. The round trench for the foundation of the dome had been dug. What a wonder to see: O. A. Jenison noted in his scrapbook, "Trench is five feet deep, fifteen feet wide and two hundred feet in circumference on the outer side."

Far more interest in print, however, was shown in the upcoming cornerstone ceremony. Requests were pouring in for permission to include mementos. There was not much space. On September 5 the *Lansing State Republican* reported that the cavity in the granite block was only sixteen inches square and twelve inches deep. A glass-lined copper box was being made to fit the hole exactly. Already the list of contents was long. Obviously they would include a copy of the Declaration of Independence. There were also special artifacts: Allen Bours had obtained parchment and written a history of Michigan with his pen, not stopping until he had filled 102 pages; the Masons, who would conduct the actual cornerstone ceremony, had contributed various Masonic papers, including the Transactions of the Grand Lodge of Michigan for 1873; the secretary of state had offered the original quill pen used to sign the first constitution of Michigan. Someone presented a copy of the *Transactions of the State Medical Society,* just off the press.

As the ceremony drew near, the list would be extended to include a copy of the Bible; the contents of the cornerstone of the first state capitol of Michigan, commenced at Detroit in 1823; an autographed copy of the legislative manual for the years 1871 and 1873; copies of all the daily newspapers of the state, specially printed on bond paper; examples of gold coins of the time; a copy of specifications for the building; copies of the laws pertaining to the building of the capitol; and blanks of official printed forms

Stonecutter Eban McPhee perches proudly atop the cornerstone with the tools of his trade. The cornerstone had arrived in Lansing only a few days before. When it was discovered that a cavity in the cornerstone intended for a glass and copper box of historic artifacts was too small, stonecutters were called in at the last moment to enlarge it.

*State Archives of Michigan*

used by the building commissioners. John Greusel donated a collection of copper pennies, while O. A. Jenison gave a set of silver, nickel, and copper coins dated 1873.

There was tremendous excitement. The commission invited the press to its last meeting before the event. Every detail was reviewed. Flags would float from the ten derricks on the building grounds. The dignitaries' platform, where the cornerstone would be placed, would stand at the northeast corner of the building (it cost $1,000!), and the muddy ground would be planked over to protect skirts and cuffs. Twenty-five to forty thousand were expected, not including all the military in the state. It was to be the greatest day Michigan had ever seen. "No pains will be spared," the *Lansing Journal* reported, "to have everything pass off decently and in order, and with becoming éclat."

The cornerstone itself arrived in town with perfect dramatic timing, on September 29. A "cheering crowd" greeted it at the station. It was then drawn by four horses up Michigan Avenue to the place where the platform had been built. Crowds thickened around it, pushing and shoving for a look inside. An official measured the cavity and to his horror it was two inches too small; stonecutters were called to the platform to chisel it larger. As they chipped away, spectators rushed forward to take the discarded chips as souvenirs.

October 2, 1873, the date finally agreed upon, proved a beautiful day for the climax of so much jubilation. It was sunny. The stores along Michigan Avenue were draped in bunting and boughs of greenery, as was the platform with the waiting cornerstone.

Cannon had been rolled up to fire and start the festivities. The historic battle flags were brought out, recalling Michigan's coming of age in triumph in the Civil War. Among these was the flag that had been captured with a fleeing Confederate president, Jefferson Davis, on a rainy day in the Georgia woods only nine years before. Many hundreds who had participated in wartime events were present.

Thirty thousand citizens were there, maybe more, but not less. They came from city, town, and farm by train and wagon, on horseback and on foot, arriving early, in good cheer. Lansing greeted them with open arms. Soldiers Restaurant advertised meals complete for fifty cents. Methodists, Presbyterians, and Episcopalians opened lunch stands. At Olin's Jewelry Store large pictures of the projected capitol were for sale for half a dollar. At noon the parade began to assemble. Various delays extended this effort, and it was two o'clock before the cannon blasted, sparking the planned festivities into motion.

The parade, a mile and a half long and led by General William Humphrey as grand marshal, moved from Washington Avenue past the old capitol, then along Ottawa Avenue to the new capitol. Before the old capitol Governor Bagley and his cabinet and guests occupied a reviewing stand. Some five thousand marched before them, Knights Templar, state militia, Masons, and Odd Fellows, among whom were twenty-five bands, playing "The Anvil Chorus," "Hail Columbia," and "Rock of Ages."

CORNERSTONE DAY WAS AS ORDERLY AND GOOD-NATURED AS A PUBLIC EVENT COULD BE.

Civil War veterans accounted for the largest number of the men marching in the parade; Orange Rison, the oldest living Freemason in the United States, is said to have kept pace. Then came the celebrated Buckskin, the horse ridden by Captain Luther Byron Baker when he captured John Wilkes Booth, Lincoln's assassin. The tall, lanky captain, frizzy with whiskers, himself never quite the attraction Buckskin was, rode him again in the parade. A descendant of Chief Okemos appeared in town that day, to the delight of old timers, who remembered the chief as a princely drop-in, complete with entourage, at settlers' picnics in days when the woods still stood.

It took an hour for the parade to reach the site of the ceremony, where the people who had watched it from the farthest away had already gathered. Twelve hundred with special tickets were admitted to the platform, where chairs were provided. The rest of the crowd spread over and beyond the boards and into the clay mud. A photographer set his lens and withdrew beneath his tent.

William Alanson Howard

State Archives of Michigan

Governor Bagley began, "Today we stand here as conquerors of forest and swamp and can proudly say, 'If thou seekest a pleasant peninsula, seek it here.'" Former Congressman William Alanson Howard, a prominent lawyer and politician and one of the state's most famous stump speakers, delivered the principal address. He recalled, "Our present state capitol was built at a cost of $22,513.02. It used to be said in derision that Governor John S. Barry paid for it by cutting and selling the hay in the capitol yard." He looked at some of his listeners, who he knew had taken part in building the old capitol. "And now these same pioneers are gathered here with upturned faces, with looks of intent and glistening eyes, to lay broad and deep the foundations of a capitol worthy of their state."

It was well received. But as the hot western sun bore down and the crowd grew restless for the main event, still the congressman talked on. After an hour he finally stepped back and took his applause. The glass-lined copper box was held up. It was placed in the cavity in the stone and the top put in place. Workmen now cranked the derricks that lifted the great stone twelve feet in the air. The crowd gasped as the huge thing moved slightly; the derrick pivoted the stone to the wall and lowered it in place in three downward motions. At each the artillery fired its rifles and the crowd cheered. Members of the Masonic order stepped forward and performed the ancient ceremony of setting the stone, working the trowel, reading the traditional speeches from their book. When at last the cornerstone was mortared in place, the crowd sang "Old Hundred."

What a day it had been. Some rowdiness usually breaks out in crowds so large and merry. Anticipating this, detectives came from Detroit to assure control. They found no work. Cornerstone day was as orderly and good-natured as a public event could be. Criticisms appeared in the press in the days that followed, notably a false accusation that women were not admitted to the platform. A state official argued that it was not true, observing that half the people on the platform were female. Governor Bagley was accused of wanting to channel some of the commission's money to his "wild parties." No one seemed to believe this. Elijah Myers, who had been front and center, had no complaints. Much of the attention had gone to him, and it may have been his most glorious day.

CHAPMAN HOUSE

In this 1887 view of Lansing, the capitol, equivalent to an eight-story building, dominates the skyline. Over 420 feet long, 273 feet wide, and 267 feet high, the capitol became known as the "Lion of Lansing."

*State Archives of Michigan*

The capitol, though only as far along as foundation walls, now had a formal identity. In the five years that followed, though it was still only growing into a finished building, the "new capitol" would be a reality in the minds of the citizens. The familiar east view, drawn by Myers with great precision of detail, was widely available to frame and hang in office and parlor. The capitol was only a great footprint in stone set into the mud of the square, but the image was portable, on paper, and it seems to have been everywhere, already moving into the iconography of daily life.

Nehemiah Osburn shut down the work with the first freeze in November 1873 and, after all set stone and brickwork were safely housed in temporary clothing of wood and straw, headed back to Rochester for the winter. In December a correspondent for the *Michigan Freemason* was shown the construction site by Myers and perhaps Appleyard or Richard Glaister. His interest for his readers was naturally in the stonework. They first inspected the "machinery and other instruments for cutting, dressing, and handling the stone of the capitol building."

Now they walked among the stones, Elijah Myers explaining the various stages from raw stone to finished stone, from the smooth-edged, rectangular blocks, or ashlar stones, for flat wall surfaces, to stones left with rough parts to be carved as ornamentation. The correspondent found stones "hewn and unhewn, rough ashlars and perfect ashlars, accepted and rejected stone. On one side, scattered about the capitol grounds, and covering acres of surface, were the huge rough stones waiting the will of the master and tool of the workman; on the other, in orderly and systematic arrangement, were perfect ashlars, and stones not ashlars but of single form and beauty. Each cut stone, 'numbered' to indicate its place in the political temple, had been inspected; not only when as a rough ashlar it was first presented, but again, after it had become under skillful hands, the perfect ashlar." Stones not suitable to use were marked "R" for "rejected," a particular fascination to the Masonic visitor.

Why was each rejected? Myers was the genial docent, with a "quick, practical eye." He pointed out with a "nervous finger" the shortcomings of each. One had a vein of ore that would grow into an ugly stain with exposure to the weather; another had a flaw that could not be corrected, so that it could never be smooth; another was a stone so porous that it was "unfitted" for "any noble purpose." In the withered weeds were stones the correspondent thought beautiful, but they were marked with the "fatal R." Myers showed their imperfections, no matter how subtle. Most of these suffered from workmen's errors. The correspondent left pleased, even delighted. Even with only a foundation to judge from, he found "strength" and "beauty."

Work was continuing in the stonemasons' lodge, with its wood stoves. At the long tables the

...THOUGH IT WAS STILL ONLY GROWING INTO A FINISHED BUILDING, THE "NEW CAPITOL" WOULD BE A REALITY IN THE MINDS OF THE CITIZENS.

Ionic and Corinthian pilasters on the capitol's exterior

*Top: The Christman Company*
*Bottom: Photo by Thomas Gennara*

stonecutters were forming column capitals in the Ionic, Doric, and Corinthian forms of ancient architecture. The lodge would be closed from Christmas until the second week in January, but the enormous challenge of creating fine finished work would keep it open as much around the calendar as possible. Most of the stonemasons appear to have been Scots, as had been typical in the stone trades in the United States since the late eighteenth century. The payrolls are lost, but the names and the few individuals, like Eban McPhee, about whom biographical information is known, point to the Scottish heritage of the capitol's lodge.

Amherst stone is a sandstone of dense quality, but like most sandstone it lacks the durability of the best limestone. It is easier than limestone to carve; easier than marble to square. Amherst stone was prized for its color, a rich buff with a very slight violet hue that is expressed in certain nuances of light. By contract the stone was quarried and delivered before the capitol commission paid the bill. It arrived at the stonemasons' lodge in rectangular blocks, rugged, or "quarry-faced," which meant that they had been only rough-shaped with chisels at the quarry.

They were inspected as laid out on the ground in the stone yard, the inferior blocks rejected. The chief stonemason now took his iron rod and wooden mallet and tapped the chosen stones to further prove their usefulness; another culling was made, after which all the rejected stones were removed, to be crushed or broken for fill. The stones that remained were now categorized by size or color as suited to various aspects of the work, and they were marked accordingly and separated. Carefully protected behind wooden fences, the fine sandstone, having thus passed muster, awaited cutting and carving.

Stonecutting was not entirely by hand. Since early in the century machines had been used to saw away quarry faces and make smooth stones. They needed strong power, and sometimes incorporated the flow of a stream, at other times horses or oxen; cogs and wheels increased the energy that turned the saws. In the 1840s dark-colored industrial diamonds made their appearance on the edge of the saws, increasing accuracy and speed. Already by the Civil War steam was the most common source of energy for stonecutting machines, and it was used in the Michigan stone yard.

Nine derricks hoisted the stones from the stone yard to the stone lodge and finally onto the table, in line for the steam machine. Stonemasons moved the stones through the machines, carefully supervising the process, studying large charcoal drawings made by the chief stonemason of what the final stone must look like, diverting the saws at intervals to study the progress of the stone and assuring accuracy of size by means of rules and calipers. The most difficult grinding and polishing were accomplished by steam power, with large, cast-iron "rubbing plates" that spun over the surface of the stone. Simpler polishing of more advanced stones was performed by a whetstone, used similarly.

Most of the stones in the capitol were probably introduced to the steam machines at some stage in their dressing, but the advantage of the machine was not so great that it made lackeys of the masons.

Far from it. No machine at that time could produce ashlar by its own effort, and the ashlar walls of the Michigan capitol are very fine. Neither was intricate carving the work of the machine, and the capitol is richly carved. What the machine did was cut the stone down further from its quarry condition to the point where handwork took over for the final finish.

> AMHERST STONE WAS PRIZED FOR ITS COLOR, A RICH BUFF WITH A VERY SLIGHT VIOLET HUE THAT IS EXPRESSED IN CERTAIN NUANCES OF LIGHT.

In January 1874 there were twenty-five stonemasons among the winter crew of fifty. The number more than doubled in the spring when work resumed full scale. Some tables apart from the machines were reserved for the carvers. Many but not all stonemasons were carvers. Carving was an art all its own, in which the artisan had to know first whether the stone would take the work planned for it. The stone came to him cut to the level and shape he needed: for a rose, a jagged lozenge protruding from a semismooth surface; for a decorative border, a rectangle, perhaps rather wide, with an unfinished mass protruding from its face. These "blanks" were carved by hand, with a variety of chisels and wooden-headed hammers of several different weights.

When Nehemiah Osburn returned to Lansing, the last freeze seemed to have passed, and on April 1 he ordered the protective covering of the completed masonry removed to look for intrusions of ice. He ordered his foreman, E. J. Green, whom he had brought from Rochester, to begin hiring bricklayers for the brickwork that would back the stone. Workmen of every sort were in town, hearing of possible work. They were taken on, it would appear, in small groups, and by the end of the month some 150 were at work. Osburn's objective was to lay five million bricks by the close of the building season in the fall. The building stood at the first level that would be exposed above the ground. Already in May the basement, or ground-floor, entrances were under way.

The capitol seemed now to be more of brick than stone. Brickwork naturally went faster, and the thick cross-walls rose in a hurry; the lining of the outside walls rose ahead of the stone to which it would be tied. Hall's brickyard outside Lansing had become quite an attraction, not only because of its connection to the capitol, but also because the public admired the entrepreneurial bravado of its youthful owner. At the yards the clay was mixed, molded, and fired. From there the bricks moved in straw-cushioned stacks directly to the building site, where laborers unloaded them on the platform, and the bricklayers' assistants took them in wheelbarrows to the parts of the building where the bricklayers were working.

The restored steps and portico of the main entrance to the capitol. In the soft light of dusk the subtle violet hue of the buff Amherst, Ohio, sandstone is clearly visible.
*Photo by Balthazar Korab*

> THERE WAS NO PARTICULAR EFFORT TO MAKE THE BRICKWORK ATTRACTIVE, BUT RESTORERS WHO EXPOSED IT AGAIN MORE THAN A CENTURY LATER WOULD MARVEL AT ITS BEAUTY.

THERE WAS NO PARTICULAR EFFORT TO MAKE THE BRICKWORK ATTRACTIVE, BUT RESTORERS WHO EXPOSED IT AGAIN MORE THAN A CENTURY LATER WOULD MARVEL AT ITS BEAUTY.

The outside walls were laid in what is usually called "American bond," meaning alternating or staggered rows, with every fifth row a "header" row, in which the bricks are turned ninety degrees, heads facing out, to link behind into a second wall adjacent, thus binding the two thicknesses together. This system was expanded to make walls three and four bricks thick. None of the work was meant to be exposed to view or to the weather. Brick, historically beloved by Americans as the permanent alternative to wood, did not satisfy those who built for the ages, and the capitol was to endure for all time. Here, brick was to play only a secondary role. Though brickmasons' work would make up the bulk of the structure, any brickwork not covered by stone on the exterior would be inside and plastered. So the mortar joints, though they had to be neatly made, could be thick, as they would never face rain or snow. Brick would back the outside walls, create interior partitions, form arches that were doorways and shallow arches that supported the floors. The rosy bricks would rise from a cylindrical base with walls fifteen feet thick, on up through the building, to support the iron dome. Yet they would not be seen. There was no particular effort to make the brickwork attractive, for there was no need to, but restorers who exposed it again more than a century later would marvel at its beauty.

The labors of April 1874 moved rapidly. Enough stone was dressed to build the basement and the first story. Very suddenly, on the evening of the 23rd, the stonecutters assembled to protest their pay; on the 27th they went on strike in protest against low wages. They had prepared a petition and selected three of their own to present it to James Appleyard. Because the commissioners had to adjust to the times—the ravages of the Panic of 1873—they cut wages of $3.75 per day in 1873 to $3.25 per day in the next year's working season. The cutters demanded a return to $3.75. Discussion seems to have been brief. The request was declined. Richard Glaister told the press that the masons were making wages about the same as those paid in Cleveland, Detroit, and other cities. They had been kept working through the past winter, which was certainly a favor to them. In any case, enough stone was cut for the time. Let them quit.

In council the stonecutters, now angry, determined that twenty of them would strike. This would not stop the work entirely but would be a fist in the belly to any great progress. Work could continue at the carving tables, because the stonemasons did not share in the strike. Setting continued on the walls. The strike lasted a few days, with the contractors refusing to budge. Finally some of the stonecutters quit and moved on, and the others returned to work.

Capitol workmen pose for the photographer around 1875. During periods of peak activity up to 225 men and boys, many skilled craftsmen, were employed. Newspapers closely followed the construction of the capitol, providing a fascinating glimpse of the building practices and trades of the day.

*State Archives of Michigan*

The capitol circa 1875. In May 1875 the *Lansing State Republican* noted with satisfaction, "The walls...begin to loom up prodigiously."

*State Archives of Michigan*

Management offered no compromise. For the time the stoneworkers were reduced to thirty. The number would be increased in the following year.

The building was taking shape. Elijah Myers liked to talk to the newsmen who occasionally passed by, looking for a story. He implied in mid-May 1874 that the public need not fear any bad results of the strike, that the walls were laid "without a fault" and would continue in that way. He went on to say that perfection was the goal. A commissioner expressed displeasure at one completed wall, and an obliging Myers ordered it demolished and rebuilt. When the commissioner went to see the new wall, he "pronounced it perfect." Myers assured everyone that the construction and finish of the building would be "unrivaled." On May 29, O. A. Jenison noted that a temporary stone that protected the cornerstone was removed at 9:10 a.m., that the first sandstone was laid on the cornerstone "and fully and firmly set at 9:50 o'clock a.m.," and that the first block of sandstone on the east side of the cornerstone was set at 10:30. Finish stonework was under way. Two months later the walls would be built on the south side up to the base of the first floor.

The purchase of lumber had begun, and lumber was being stacked in the sheds near the carpenters' hall. Of all the materials used in the new capitol, wood was the one Michigan could provide with the greatest ease and excellence. For the capitol rose in the halcyon days of the timber industry, when the Lower Peninsula was being logged with axes, saws, skidders, and trams. It seemed that the supply of forest trees could never end; to any objection to the pillage, a woodsman might respond that the end would be so distant, who could care? It was the pioneer spirit, in all its virility and destructiveness. No more appropriate use could there be for some of this wood than in building the state's new capitol. The lumber, brought down from the north, came on the train, like everything else. Myers specified Norway pine for work that would not be seen, although what was uncovered by restorers in the 1980s seems to have been simply Michigan white pine. This arrived at the site already milled as lumber in three ways: smooth on one side and three inches wide and one and one-eighth inches thick for flooring, and as rough studs two inches by six inches and two by four, to fix to the brick interior walls and ceilings as backing for lath and plaster. It was ordered to be "clear of all knots, sap, wind-shakes, or defects." The specifications controlled even the logging process: After cutting, the logs were to be piled up "on the grounds under cover" for two years before being "worked," or milled, for the capitol. After over a century in place in the capitol, the Michigan pine was still to retain the sweet smell of the northern forests.

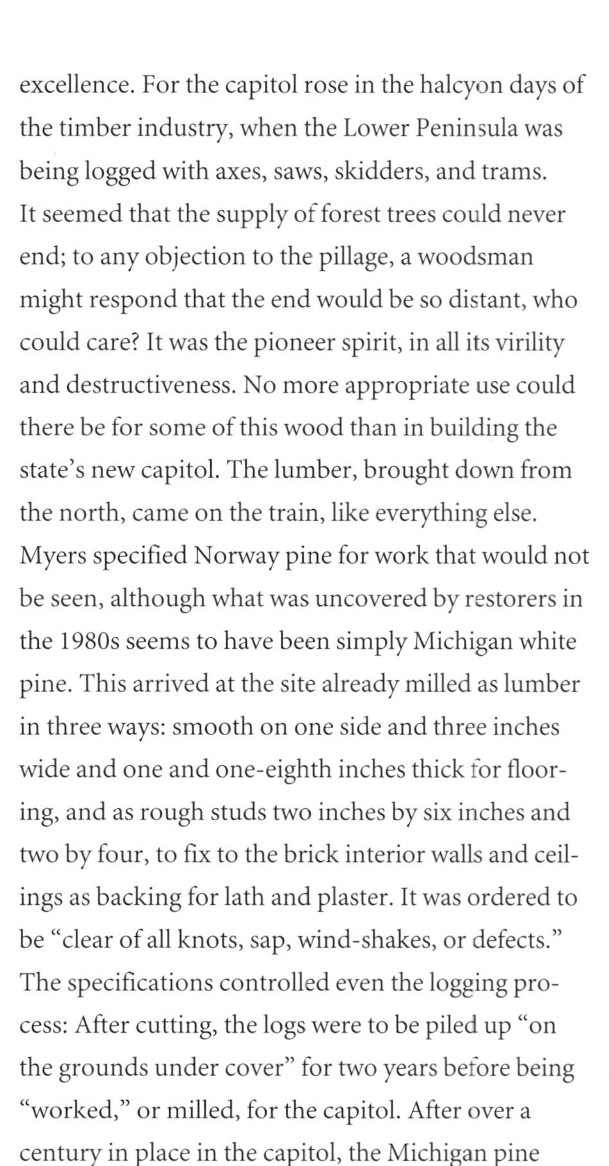

AFTER OVER A CENTURY IN PLACE IN THE CAPITOL, THE MICHIGAN PINE WAS STILL TO RETAIN THE SWEET SMELL OF THE NORTHERN FORESTS.

This was only a part of the wood to be used, for a particular splendor of the capitol was to be its abundant display of finished black walnut, one of the princely products of Michigan's coldest forest zones. The actual material, however, being so costly and widely desirable for furniture in that "walnut age," would be used

To save money, walnut was specified for use only in certain locations, such as the Senate chamber rostrum, shown here. Elsewhere, skillfully painted pine closely mimicked the appearance of walnut at a fraction of the cost.

*Photo by Balthazar Korab*

only in the offices of the governor, lieutenant governor, and Speaker of the House, in the rostrums of the chambers, and in the bench of the Supreme Court. Elsewhere, Myers specified that "English branch walnut" be imitated through a paint technique over white pine. As it happened, the graining imitated black walnut instead, and the use of actual black walnut extended to major furnishings and cabinetry, all designed by Myers as part of the original capitol scheme.

As far as wood structure was concerned, traditional timber-frame, or joined, construction was not used here. Iron had taken its place in engineering, and Elijah Myers would have greatly increased the quantity used, had not the commissioners curbed his enthusiasm. While the steel frame was still some years away in building history, the use of wrought iron in the wooden skeleton of a building was common. Introduced in England in the late eighteenth century, wrought-iron members had generally been replaced fifty years later by cast iron, which had changed the character of major construction. Myers seems to have been up with the latest technology. The completed capitol would boast 1,400,700 pounds of iron floor beams, 230,000 pounds of iron roof trusses, and 19,717 pounds of iron tie rods, anchors, and securing fixtures. The dome trusses would weigh 170 tons; the iron stairs, columns, and other cast-iron architectural features inside, 674,464 pounds; the iron plate smokestack that vented the basement's steam boilers, 61,050 pounds. The result was a total of 2,725,931 pounds of cast iron, not counting the corrugated metal covering the roof's 467,700 square feet. Adding to this the weight of brick and stone, the capitol was a very heavy load on the Michigan earth, weighing perhaps three times what a modern ten-story steel-frame building of comparable volume would total.

Cast iron was used in many ways, some visible and ornamental, others structural and unseen. The latter elements were predominantly single beams, or girders, composed of two or more parts bolted together. The iron beams, which were rather like the I beams we know today, varied from six to eight to twelve inches top to bottom, and rode usually on brick walls, supporting what was above. Where there were large open spaces, as in the great corridors, Myers designed iron columns to bear the load. Extra support columns were sometimes used in areas such as the auditor general's office, where heavy files or equipment might be extensive.

The floors, beneath the wood or marble, were beds of iron and masonry. There was some discussion at commission meetings about the high cost of supporting the floors, and Myers came up with a practical solution of combining iron and brick. Cast-iron beams, placed on four- to six-foot centers, were spanned by brick jack arches—the term meaning in this case simply a low, rough, barrel-like structural arch not meant to be seen—forming shallow vaults beam to beam that were considered to be fireproof. Corrugated sheet iron, appropriately bent to the necessary shapes, provided security and fireproofing behind plastered walls in several areas. The iron in the capitol came from two different sources, the cast iron and girders from Samuel J. Creswell, Philadelphia, and

Brick jack arches, supported by iron beams, span the brick walls and form the floors throughout the capitol. Infill was added above to provide level surfaces and fireproofing; lath and plaster were added below to create flat ceilings. Only in the ground-floor corridor ceilings were the jack arches left undisguised.

*Photo by Thomas Gennara*

THE CAPITOL WAS A VERY HEAVY LOAD ON THE MICHIGAN EARTH, WEIGHING PERHAPS THREE TIMES WHAT A MODERN TEN-STORY STEEL-FRAME BUILDING OF COMPARABLE VOLUME WOULD TOTAL.

the galvanized iron from John Siddons of Rochester, New York.

Racing against the coming winter, Osburn pressed the work of 1874 to such an extent that the first floor was nearly completed in October and stones were set in the second floor. The some two hundred workmen labored hard and, as evidence of this, also played hard. Activities they enjoyed can be traced in the local newspapers of their time. They went hunting in the countryside around the town, held subscription dances, and attended lectures, performances at the opera house, and Lansing's many churches. The little city had its share of attractions. Theatrical road companies performed there regularly. In 1875 the Baker Family performed the *Oratorio of the Court of Babylon*, assisted by sixty Lansing singers. That great though as yet unexposed hoax, the Cardiff Giant, arrived by train the same year, and hundreds paid to look in wonder on his stony face. Some spent their wages in the town's numerous saloons. For construction tradesmen hours were long and work was hard, and saloon life led to casualties in a few shootings and to some arrests for public drunkenness. This seems not to have been typical, however. Most of the workmen seem to have been a sober, dedicated lot.

During the winter cold weather forced construction to a virtual standstill, as seen in this December 1874 photograph.
*State Archives of Michigan*

When the push relaxed and parts of the job were stopped until spring, the stonecutters, as usual, emerged triumphant, with at least twenty-five assured of work in the lodge all winter. Closed in by four protective walls and warmed by wood stoves, they continued at their machines into the winter of 1875, which proved fierce. The pipes that brought water to the machines froze in their shallow ditches, and only with bonfires were Osburn's people able to thaw them out so that work might continue.

Winter was a strange time at the building site. The somnolent, gray days, with leaden skies, varied by snowfall and long periods of freezing, were milder than in most parts of Michigan but too severe to allow for any building activity that would expose materials, particularly masonry, to moisture. Progress sounded only from the stonemasons' lodge in the roaring and grinding of the steam machine and the occasional yelling of commands down the benches. The building was packed in straw and boarded up haphazardly but tightly where there was work from the previous season, to protect it from ice and snow, and it looked odd and formidable. Once the work of covering had been loosely handled by the New York workmen of Nehemiah Osburn, and serious damage was the result. Every precaution was taken now. Open sheds were closed in where necessary and all parts of the machinery but the main shafts, which were kept inside, were dismantled, the vulnerable sections stored under cover.

We know little of what happened to the workmen in the following season. Only the few who remained at work were paid. No compensation of any kind awaited those who were told they were not needed before the following spring; Tuesday payday for them was no more. These were not good times. The Panic of 1873, which had begun in the East, was being felt in the Midwest. The warmer South was not yet recovered sufficiently from the war to offer much alternate opportunity. Evidence suggests that the workmen did the best they could do and stayed in Lansing. Perhaps some of the young boys on the job,

THE WORK HAD NEVER GONE FORWARD SO VIGOROUSLY AS IT DID IN THE SEASON OF 1875.

like eleven-year-old Willie Green, who operated a steam derrick, went to school. Nor was the resumption of work always predictable. The site did not reopen until the frost had left the ground, and sometimes this was well into April. On the second of that month in 1875 the frost, according to the *Lansing State Republican*, was still six feet four inches down from the surface. Work could not resume for seventeen days. Even so, on April 22 the commissioners ordered the work to cease, for they believed frost was still present.

The legislature made additional appropriations in 1875 to improve the proposed heating system and make better steps to the north, east, and south porticoes, as well as to enhance the interior finish. In April an appropriation was made for a roof of Michigan copper. Answering pressures from all sides, that same month the legislature allowed $65,000 to pay for a stone cornice and balustrade, instead of the painted tin Myers had originally proposed. Meanwhile, the contractors protested the board's stoppage of the work because of the frost, and the work took up again.

The season of 1875 had its tensions. Although a generous legislature looked favorably on the new capitol, the national financial panic made its mark in hot tempers as well as empty pocketbooks. Allen Bours came under increasing criticism not only because of his gruff manner, but also for holding other state jobs while he worked on the capitol. He seems to have done his work well, but he made enemies. At last George P. Sanford, editor of the *Lansing Journal*, attacked the secretary in print. The two had clashed before on personal matters. Now Sanford's articles accused him of double dealing.

Bours was enraged. He had said before that if he had much more trouble with Sanford he would horsewhip him, which, when Sanford persisted in his articles, was exactly what he did. With a friend, Bours called at the *Journal*'s office. While the friend waited on the sidewalk, Bours entered, withdrew his riding whip from his coat, and beat Sanford's "hat" and "shoulder"—or, at least, so he claimed later. What actually happened is not clear, as the two parties told different stories. Bours said that the editor struggled with him, then took an iron poker from the stove to defend himself, and Bours left. Whatever the truth, the inevitable assault charges followed, as an angry Sanford pursued his assailant by legal means. Unable to resist, the *Journal*'s rival, the *Lansing State Republican,* quipped: "The editor of the *Journal* still claims that he held so good a hand in poker that Mr. Bours was obliged to pass—out of doors." The conclusion after two separate court trials was that Bours paid a $25 fine.

The work had never gone forward so vigorously as it did in the season of 1875. Two hundred twenty hands reported when the steam whistle sounded at seven in the morning, and work sometimes continued into the night. A puckish reporter for the Leslie, Michigan, *Herald* walked over the building site and wrote down his impressions of the workmen. Through the crowded yards he wandered, listening to the talk and joking, much of it about the panic and hard times: "Joers, now min," said a bricklayer, presumably Irish, "meself is going to quit work for the banking business—shoveling sand is asier than this."

The reporter found that they worked "on the edge of death," carrying their hods of mortar up and down, along plank walks placed high. "It makes me dizzy to look down from the height where many of

The recently-completed east portico and stairs, circa 1878. A projecting four-story central pavilion, capped by a triangular pediment, features a two-story colonnaded porch and broad stairs, clearly indicating the capitol's ceremonial main entrance.

*State Archives of Michigan*

them work and smoke and laugh. One man stood on a foot wide parapet adjusting a big stone with his back to a sheer down height from which one misstep or trip would plunge him to instant death. We hinted danger when he took a pipe from his mouth and laughed a jolly big laugh at the thought of such a thing." While there were no surprises that day, workmen did fall from time to time, suffering cuts and bruises and occasionally broken bones, and one Thomas Zamosky eventually died of injuries from a fall.

In the commissioners' office the officials and Osburn came to terms over the additions ordered by the legislature. The stone cornice and balustrade were agreed upon, as well as the erection of more important steps to the east or principal front of the building. Myers's original cornice design was simply to be made in stone rather than pressed tin. The stairs to the columned east porch were another matter. These were given to the architect to redesign entirely, and he produced a grand design indeed, one with a broad intermediate landing approached three ways, then stairs on up to the porch. It was given elaborate carved newels and heavy balustrades, and provided a gentle, even luxurious ascent. As for the roof of Michigan copper, this was reviewed in some detail and cast out as too costly, in favor of the tin originally proposed.

Elijah Myers reviewed what must have seemed endless samples of glass, walnut, bronze, and stone sent by mail or brought by company agents. Those he approved he laid before the commissioners for final acceptance, although on any subject the commissioners were likely to intervene, taking full and active parts. They questioned Myers and Appleyard extensively, for their own familiarity with the building business made them exacting clients. Bid openings were very serious times, with all commissioners always present, and the governor nearly always there. They informed the press from such a united front that their deliberations seemed smooth and peaceful. Very often the press was invited to their meetings. If discord occasionally marred progress, it was hidden well behind closed doors and not resolved publicly.

Considerable time was given to modern conveniences, at least as those were known at the time: heating, lighting, ventilation, and sanitation. These were subjects of great interest everywhere, and particularly in Lansing, as the old capitol's inadequacies for simple use were many. Already the legislature had been heard on the subject of heat and had appropriated an additional $70,000 to pay for the best steam heating, with radiators. The concept of heating with pipes filled with steam, known vaguely since the 1830s, had come into its own in the 1850s and was in a nearly constant state of improvement. Steam heat was more desirable than the gravity air system then used in houses, for it required no fireplaces to create drafts and move the air, but heated interiors by means of steam moving through iron pipes. Precautions had to be taken to drain off condensation, and escape valves warded off boiler explosions of the kind that haunted steamboats on the rivers.

A closeup view of the tympanum over the entrance portico reveals details of the only sculpture ever to decorate the capitol. Sometimes called *The Rise and Progress of Michigan*, the work symbolizes Michigan's transformation from wilderness to a modern agricultural and industrial state. For many, the capitol itself stood as a powerful symbol of their belief in Michigan's future.

*Photo by Dietrich Floeter*

Michigan's capitol commissioners ordered the huge steam boilers put beneath the porticoes, so that, if they blew up, the body of the building would be saved. Myers had ideas of his own about steam heating and even made a worthy innovation in the introduction of individual air ducts—really small grooves in the wall—that brought fresh air from outside to each radiator.

The plan included a very extensive sanitation system with surprisingly numerous toilet rooms, equipped with hot water, for both the officials and the public. Women's rooms were where women would be, near the visitors' galleries to the chambers; all others were for men. Some offices had washbasins in addition. As for light, gas was always to be the source, to supplement the daylight that would flood every floor. Gray midwestern days would require artificial light sometimes during working hours, in spite of abundant windows and skylights. In 1876 it was decided to equip the capitol with a battery-operated electrical system, not for light—for it was yet three years before Edison's electric lights—but to spark the gas fixtures in the major and tallest spaces, the rotunda, chambers, state library, Supreme Court, and corridors. In all other areas the gas was lighted with matches.

Ventilation was the issue of the day in American public buildings for at least twenty years. A letter to the editor of the *Lansing State Republican* observed, "There is a closer connection between bad air and bad legislation than people imagine." Every legislature in the country had become concerned about the air it breathed. Michigan's lawmakers informed the architect and contractor in January 1875 that they wished to "have the best and most perfect ventilation system in every room and every corner" of the new building. The widespread use of gravity air central heating systems had first appeared in state capitols in the 1840s, making legislative chambers dry and stale, nearly suffocating. Deliberations over ventilation during the expansion of the United States Capitol had brought the subject to universal attention. The decision in Washington was to move steam-heated air into the rooms with steam-operated fans. For Michigan, steam heating through pipes run into the rooms was a first measure toward better air. An extensive ventilation system for removing "foul air" seems to have done the rest. Numerous brick shafts were cut from rooms up through the walls into roof ventilators; airflow was adjusted by louvers. Under the careful monitoring of the legislators, the ventilation system was carried out to the fullest, the beginnings of its installation seen in the earliest brickwork.

Among the embellishments the commissioners approved in the winter of 1876 were the carvings for the eastern tympanum, or the inner, triangular section of the pediment that projected on the highest part of the roof, just below the base of the dome. A Detroit sculptor, Herman Wehner, had been employed to make a model in plaster for the board's approval, and this was presented to them on January 25, 1876. Wehner worked in a room in the capitol, presumably a first-floor room on one of the north corners that had been temporarily closed in as a studio, and here he prepared a half-scale model in plaster of what he proposed for the tympanum. First the commissioners, then interested legislators came to inspect.

Wehner, invited to the job, had come to Michigan with his family from Prussia as a child. As a youth he had worked as a mill hand to help support his widowed mother. When he showed a proclivity for carving, he attracted the attention of a rich patron, who arranged for him to study in Newburgh, New York, under Henry Kirke Brown, the Massachusetts-born sculptor of the equestrian George Washington in

Union Square, New York, still considered Manhattan's most successful piece of outdoor sculpture. Only two years before, in 1874, Brown had completed the equestrian statue of General Winfield Scott at Scott Circle, Washington, D.C., cast from bronze cannon captured during the Mexican War. Wehner may well have worked on this while an apprentice in Brown's New York studio.

Three details of the finished tympanum. Michigan herself strides from the wilderness, offering a book and globe—symbols of progress—to her people (top). A cornucopia and sheaf of wheat symbolize agriculture (middle). Ore and tools symbolize the state's mining industry (bottom).

*Photos by Thomas Gennara*

Wehner's initial plaster model for the capitol project featured a Native American woman, representing Michigan, standing in the center, with shield and dagger. To her left was the famous "boy governor," Stevens T. Mason, elected to Michigan's highest office in 1835 at the age of twenty four; on her right, on a log from a fallen tree, the hardy pioneer, with his ox, symbolizing both the settler and the lumber industry. The composition incorporated a sheaf of wheat, symbolizing agriculture; a stack of books and a globe, for advanced education in the state; a pick and spade to show mining; and a schooner and locomotive for commerce. A reporter praised the "suggestive beauty and harmony" of this composition. Others, perhaps including the commissioners, felt differently.

Lewis T. Ives, of Detroit, produced a rival cartoon, or sketch, of a simpler, more direct concept. He used many of Wehner's ideas; in fact, he had probably consulted with Wehner. His grouping was of three female figures, a standing Michigan flanked by the seated Agriculture and Commerce. Plows, pickaxes, and other tools to support the themes were placed about their feet. This approach seemed to suit everybody, so Wehner was directed to follow Ives's cartoon. (The design was referred to on occasion as being by Wehner and Ives, but the commissioners' contract was with Wehner alone.) In the final version the central figure is a female in Native American regalia, resolute to show that she, Civilization, is emerging from the wilderness era of Michigan and heralds a glorious future.

Concerned perhaps with their isolation on this project, the commissioners decided to make a trip east to inspect buildings. Heating and lighting were their announced interests. At the end of April and for most of May 1876 they traveled to inspect the latest major building projects in the East. They wished to see many sorts of things relevant to the new capitol, but in particular they were concerned about electrically ignited gaslight systems. Departing by train from Detroit, they went to New York City, where they visited twenty buildings, including Tammany Hall, the fanciful headquarters of the Democratic Party's Tammany Society. The concert halls of the Steinway and Chickering piano companies offered the finest in gas lighting. From New York the commissioners went down to Philadelphia to see the Centennial Exposition, celebrating the one hundredth anniversary of the Declaration of Independence. There they found Michigan much in evidence in a display of fashionable furniture produced in Grand Rapids, but more so in an exhibit of giant logs brought from the northern forests. At the exposition's close, S. J. Creswell, the Philadelphia manufacturer of cast iron stairs, columns, and other elements for the capitol in Lansing, purchased the Michigan logs to use in forming his castings.

The centennial was the last important public ceremony in Lansing not to take place in the new capitol.

Home on the last day of May, the commissioners seem to have been happy with what they had seen on their trip, for they held a meeting in Lansing and approved the electric igniting system for the capitol. To this had been added an electric annunciation device, whereby from any office an official could summon the building's engineer or janitor with the press of a button. It worked like a servants' bell system in a private home or a hotel: A call box would locate the source of the ring by the drop of a lever representing the particular room.

The commissioners were pleased to find parts of the balustrade being installed along the edge of the roof. Inside, the steam heating apparatus was being put in place. With 125 men at work, the walls rose fast, and the balustrade was installed as soon as the cornice was set. On the Fourth of July the national centennial was celebrated in Lansing with parades and orations. Everyone attended, and not a stone was laid on the capitol. Citizens crowded to New Hope Cemetery to the temporary monument of wood, covered with granite paper, to remember those who had sacrificed their lives in the war. For never a day could pass, nor an oration sound, nor a memory be kindled that it was not dominated by the Civil War. It was Michigan's war, Michigan's win. At the old capitol the Women's Monument Association had decorated "gaily with flags, wreaths, and flowers." Apropos the idea of age, relics of history were amassed for the thousands to see, a sword captured on the battlefield of Waterloo, many china dishes "100 to 300 years old," an old powder flask (many could even remember ones like it), a wooden bowl made in 1730, and "lamps from Pompeii, 1,900 years old."

The centennial was the last important public ceremony in Lansing not to take place in the new capitol. For all times after, the capitol would be the stage or at least the background for such events. At this point its horizontal form appeared almost complete from Michigan Avenue, end to end, ground to cornice. Sixteen days after the centennial, the first iron parts of the dome arrived in Lansing. That autumn, against the skeletal beginnings of the rising dome, the carvings of the tympanum were lifted to the pediment and mortared into place. O. A. Jenison wrote in his scrapbook that the center figure rested in position on Wednesday, October 4, 1876, at 4:30 p.m. "The piece containing the globe at her right was placed in position just one hour afterwards. The piece at her left was placed in position at 8:30 o'clock in the morning of October 5, 1876."

Fellow spectators who saw Jenison's pencil fly over the paper knew who he was and why he wrote: The whole community recognized his role as the chronicler of the new capitol. Oddly, Jenison did not note the laying of the last stone in the walls, which took place on October 31. It was not a planned event. Unusually warm fall weather continued until long after the leaves were gone. Work was not stopped. The exterior columns were all cut and dressed and stacked like "saw logs" in the sheds, themselves to be closed in for winter. Workmen were being laid off until spring. The last stone might have made a dramatic conclusion to the season, but the work went on until the freeze on December 2, allowing time to carry the roof near completion.

Rising above the city it would soon dominate, the dome under construction presented an unforgettable sight. This 1877 view shows one of the capitol's few rivals for the Lansing skyline, the Plymouth Congregational Church to the south.

*State Archives of Michigan*

O. A. Jenison recorded that the first piece of iron for the dome was put in place in November 1876. Photographs show the framework for the inner and outer domes. The final piece was installed on June 15, 1878.

*All: State Archives of Michigan*

Three months later the final construction season for the exterior was well under way. The dome seemed to rise daily before the eyes of the fascinated public, its iron parts coming together like the pieces of a puzzle. Stonemasons were busy building the great external stairs and porches. At the same time, finish work was commenced inside, now safe from the elements. Plasterers began nailing their lath, by mid-April were troweling the mud coat, and in May, in some parts, the final or white coat. A reporter from the *Lansing State Republican* found "large beds of sand and mortar piled up on the second floor." A ground-floor room had been set up as a studio for J. Roberts, who was making ornamental plaster decorations to crown some of the doors and embellish some of the walls.

During the summer of 1877, as the effort on the interiors was intensified, the pressed tin ornamentation for the ceilings of the legislative halls and the lantern of the dome arrived from John Siddons's manufactory in Rochester. Custom-made to Myers's designs in galvanized tin pressed to shape at the factory around wooden forms, the tinwork represented the building's most ambitious interior architectural detailing. When painted, this innovation of the age would give a rich effect for less cost and with less weight than the plaster or wood it represented. Charles Vogle was sent from Rochester to supervise the installation. The elements for the dome, which came in pieces of various sizes, were screwed to cast-iron framing on the inside and cast-iron ribbing on the outside. When the first of the tin was put up in the legislative halls, it made an almost instant transformation of barren spaces into ones of architectural magnificence.

The east grounds were cleared of debris and plowed up, and within a year a neat, open-board fence, such as one might see around a paddock, was put up along the edge of the property facing Michigan Avenue. In midsummer the *Lansing State Republican*'s chronicler made another tour with Elijah Myers. The capitol was having some political trouble; Democrats were pointing out how many Republicans had been given contracts for work on the building. Perhaps there was a story. With the architect as "courteous" and "intelligent" guide, the newsman was shown the building and was smitten. Why, it was a masterpiece! "There is not a timber, a bolt, or anything from the most ornate girder or pillar down to the smallest ornament" that had not been carefully planned. "These things cost time, labor, experience, and skill," he insisted, in the most flattering terms. Nearly a month later he wrote, "The first grand rib of the dome of the new capitol was placed in position." That took place on August 13, 1877. One hundred fifty workers pushed the capitol toward a December completion, which would ultimately be postponed ten months.

It was the rising dome that was to fascinate the public more than any other part of the building. Framed in cast iron and sided in cast-iron plates, it took shape fast, its parts precast at the Philadelphia foundry of S. J. Creswell. The manufacturer himself traveled to Lansing in the fall to see the dome in construction. Another late winter extended the work into early December, but though Nehemiah Osburn had hoped to finish by Christmas, it was not to be. The dome was stopped in December sixty-seven feet short of the 267 feet it would ultimately reach. Much of the plasterwork was complete. All the windows were in. Cast-iron staircases were all in place. Marble tiles for the great corridors were in crates inside the building.

When the cold finally came two weeks into December, the coal furnace was lighted so work could be continued inside.

As for the interior, it was well along. The cast-iron framework for the rotunda balconies was built, and the iron-plate floor panels were being installed, as well the framing which would hold the glass tiles for the rotunda floor. Finish woodwork was being delivered. The contract for this had gone to Alfred Wise, who owned a steam millwork enterprise in Lansing. Myers had designed the woodwork, but his drawings were not detailed as to construction. Through the years there had been some debate about the wood to be used, Michigan being a principal supplier of such fine cabinet woods as black walnut. The high cost of that material had restricted its use in favor of less expensive northern pine in most rooms. The pine was milled in the same form but grained by means of a layering of brown paint colors applied with brushes to imitate the striation natural to real wood grain, then covered with pigmented glazes to give the appearance of highly finished and "rubbed" black walnut.

The millwork factory was alongside the railroad tracks, where on a spur Wise received his materials when they arrived from northern Michigan. Steam-operated saws and planers in the hands of skilled employees turned out fine carpentry and millwork that are among the enduring glories of the building. Carved, incised, and enriched in some instances with panels of French branch black walnut burl (which was also simulated in painted graining), the millwork poured from the Wise shop through the months of 1877 and 1878.

*ADVERTISEMENTS.*

MITCHELL, VANCE & CO.,

NEWEST AND CHOICEST DESIGNS OF

GAS ✦ FIXTURES,

Metal and Porcelain Lamps.

*Also, Electroliers for Every System of Electric Lighting. Special Designs submitted on application.*

FINE CLOCKS,
MANTEL SETS,
ARTISTIC BRONZES.

In addition to those of our own manufacture, we offer an unequaled assortment, selected this season with great care in Paris, Vienna, Berlin, London, and other European cities.

Also, articles of ORNAMENTAL METAL WORK, both antique and modern, in great variety and elegance of workmanship.

Our rooms have been recently fitted up with special regard to the exhibition of these goods, to an inspection of which a cordial invitation is extended.

MITCHELL, VANCE & CO.,
836 and 838 Broadway, and 13th Street,
NEW YORK.

Advertisement for Mitchell, Vance & Company of New York, which manufactured many of the lighting fixtures for the capitol

*State Archives of Michigan*

This pre-1885 photograph shows one of the twenty elaborate gas chandeliers manufactured for the grand corridors. Custom-made for the capitol, they feature elk and other motifs from the state's coat-of-arms.

*State Archives of Michigan*

For a while during the winter it seemed that a Fourth of July dedication might be possible. By March it was clear that the building would not be finished. At that time bids went out for furniture and carpeting. On March 2 Allen Bours went east with the state treasurer, William B. McCreery, whose wise and shrewd ways with money had nearly liquidated Michigan's debts, and whom the commissioners would trust to make purchasing decisions on the spot. They visited gaslight fixture manufactories. Final arrangements were made with Mitchell, Vance & Company of New York City for gas fixtures for the entire building, costing a total of $8,000. The firm had been widely praised for its display at the Centennial Exposition in Philadelphia and was known for simple fixtures as well as rather outlandish ones. For a church in Aurora, Indiana, the company produced fixtures adorned with marble statuettes of Christ; for Western Union in New York it created a fantastic fixture with Grecian vases, fluted columns, lions' heads, and griffins that was, by the company's own advertisement, "one of the most elaborate designs of the kind ever executed in this country." Michigan's gas chandeliers for the grand corridors would, with their elk, state shields, and torchères, eclipse even this.

Through the summer the finish work continued. By June 15 workmen on the dome were high enough into the lantern to stick a broom out the top and fix to it the American flag. People on the street cheered to see the first flag float over the capitol. On July 19 the scaffolding was removed. Reported the press when the dome was complete: "it stands forth in all its architectural beauty." Marble and tile floors were being laid within. Doors were being hung, even as the varnishers were rubbing the surfaces of the walnut with pumice and paint grainers were varnishing over their walnut deceptions. On September 26, 1878, the commissioners met with Elijah Myers and Nehemiah Osburn, and all agreed that the building was finished. A check was made out to Osburn for $136,304.70, final payment for a job everyone agreed was well done.

The governor's parlor, where newly-sworn-in Governor Croswell greeted visitors attending dedication ceremonies for the new capitol, January 1, 1879. On November 19, 1992, 113 years later, in the same room, now restored, Governor and Mrs. John Engler greeted those attending the capitol's rededication ceremonies.

*Photo by Balthazar Korab*

## DEDICATION

The dedication and first convening of the legislature were held on New Year's Day 1879, along with the inauguration of Governor Charles Croswell for a second term in office. It was a beautiful day. Special early morning trains ran from Jonesville, Litchfield, Homer, Condit, Albion, Devereux, Springport, Charlesworth, Eaton Rapids, Kingsland, Dimondale, Packards, and South Lansing. Thousands of people poured into Lansing through the railroad station, there for the day, for the trains departed at ten at night. The town was already full when they arrived.

At seven in the morning the American flag was raised over the capitol and the doors were thrown open. By mid-morning the building was filled with visitors. High state officials stood by in their offices, receiving callers with New Year's greetings, and although they had not entirely moved in, the offices looked finished. Particularly did the governor's office, with its rich furnishings and draperies, arouse admiration. At nine o'clock the House chamber—then called the Representative Hall—was opened, and "the hall was speedily filled to the fullest capacity." The official party entered behind a band, marching across the building from the Senate chamber. Governor Croswell was seated in the great carved chair of the Speaker, flanked by Lieutenant Governor Alonzo Sessions and Bishop George D. Gillespie; below, seated in chairs lined up facing the audience, were the principal officers of the state. When the crowd settled down, the swearing in took place, and several hours' speaking began.

The formal ceremony gave in to an afternoon's and evening's merriment. By four o'clock the skies darkened, but the visitors stayed on. Governor Croswell, a widower, received with his son and daughter in the "governor's parlor." Outside the windows snow began to fall. In one of the hallways a dance had begun to music from the Knights Templar band. Electrical devices were tripped, and the gaslight spread its yellow glow over the rooms and corridors, the curled and slicked hair, the lace collars, gingham and silk, broadcloth and jean, slipper and boot. The snow started falling thickly. Still the crowds remained. Just before ten an exodus scampered down the front stairs to Michigan Avenue and ventured through the snow to the station. A later crowd departed, mostly local people and farmers, into snow that had become deep, to inch their way homeward. In the newly white landscape the capitol shone like a wonderful lantern, ablaze with light, towering above the low buildings of the town, seeming, so unlike those earthbound wooden boxes, to reach entirely into the clouds.

The capitol, winter 1992

*Photo by Michael Quillinan*

Restored, the grand corridors look much as they did in the 1880s. The crisp black and white Vermont marble tile floors and painted walls, ceilings, columns, wainscot, doors, and trim sum up the sumptuous era of the Gilded Age.

*Photo by Balthazar Korab*

Thus it was left alone that New Year's night, as are capitols every night. No one lives in them. They are stages for performances great and small, but not homes. Myers had labeled some of the ground-floor rooms of the Michigan capitol as official living quarters for the lieutenant governor, but to our knowledge it was for lack of anything else to call them. At first the idea of a lieutenant governor's apartment probably had a fleeting appeal as a means for justifying extra space. It was never used. When day was done, everyone left. The doors were locked. The capitol slept.

For a few hours in the early morning daylight was the sole inhabitant of the building, illuminating its democratic splendors. This was and still is a good time to see the capitol, without people, for its architecture and contents. Though it is certainly true that a capitol without people is like a fountain without water, the crowds that usually fill the halls make it difficult to study the building in any detail.

FOR A FEW HOURS IN THE EARLY MORNING DAYLIGHT WAS THE SOLE INHABITANT OF THE BUILDING, ILLUMINATING ITS DEMOCRATIC SPLENDORS.

The interior of the Michigan capitol is remarkable, and was remarkable. When it was first occupied, the interior's plaster walls were simply raw white, allowing for the long drying period so necessary to plaster of Paris before the introduction of modern vehicles for quick drying, and awaiting the time six years after the dedication, when an extensive program was begun of applying the present decorative treatments with paint and plaster. When that was done, the concept for the building was at last fulfilled. Any description of the early building should center in about 1890, when it was complete.

Elijah Myers's old friend Samuel Sloan would have been delighted with the interior Myers had produced. With its painted decorations, it had an exotic flavor, the vast corridors paved in black and white checkerboard marble squares, the ceilings very high and painted azure as though open to a southern sky, the walls textured in swirls and painted in imitation of Morocco leather.

This detail of a painted plaster ceiling from the main entry corridor shows how simple materials were fashioned to create a rich effect.

*Photo by Thomas Gennara*

The enveloping sense of its ornamentation was complete. As he boasted he always did, Myers had seen to every detail. The doorknobs were fine metal —"ounce metal," with an ounce of tin, an ounce of zinc, and an ounce of lead added to a pound of copper—bronze-finished and cast with the coat of arms of Michigan. Etched glass shimmered in the transoms. From the ceilings the remarkable giant "gasoliers" seemed to float as they presided over the lofty corridors, rich in ornamentation of leaves and turnings. The symbolic elk of Michigan wandered proudly on them in imitation bronze, among balloon-like lamp globes.

The legislative chambers were like opera houses, and grander than many. Much of the area of the ceilings was glass panes, etched and decorated with the coats of arms of the states of the Union; through these natural light fell through skylights from the attic onto furnishings handsomely designed by Myers in black walnut, carpets of rich color and pattern, and gaslight fixtures of brass. "Sunburst" chandeliers, which were great circular canopies lined with mirrors and spangled with cast lead crystal and glass prisms and beads, provided light on gray days and at night; but not enough light, so additional brass pendant fixtures were put along the galleries, as one sometimes saw in theaters. When the painter's brush touched the architectural shells of the rooms they were elevated to magnificence, with touches of gilt and Pompeiian coloration: lush predominant colors of cool blue-green in the Senate chamber and a bold, warm clay or terra cotta in the House chamber.

In the capitol's restored first-floor corridors, cast iron columns and pine wainscot are painted as they were originally to resemble more costly marble.

*Michigan Capitol Committee*

The Supreme Court chamber, though much smaller than the legislative halls, rivaled them in grandeur. On the east end Myers had fairly filled the entire wall with fine walnut cabinetwork, before which stood the judges' bench. Pilasters lined the walls, supporting a deep cornice. The courtroom was approached by a vestibule and adjoined by ample offices that extended to an uncovered terrace on the roof over the east porches. In its painted decorations, the room was splendid indeed, with ceilings of sky blue and motifs that suggested the Anglo-Japanese style, a feature of the popular tastes of the day, which were art-like or Aesthetic, as the term went, meaning that the designer applied the principles of fine art to the finish-ing of interiors.

Hardware for the capitol was custom made. Doorknobs and hinges were cast with the Michigan coat of arms.

*State Archives of Michigan*

An 1879 view of the governor's parlor

*State Archives of Michigan*

On the second floor, beneath the Supreme Court, was the finest office in the building, that of the governor. This included the "governor's parlor," used for the governor's receptions, a handsome, nearly cubical room approached through massive walnut doors with etched-glass panes. One of the few fireplaces in the building was here; lost for many years, it was uncovered during restoration, and its firebox showed evidence of having been used for coal. The furniture of the room was the particular pride of the capitol. Richly carved in the *néo-grec* mode of combined classical motifs, the suite consisted of a tall, eagle-mounted sideboard, cabinet, and table, together with upholstered armchairs. None of it was designed by Myers. The case pieces and table were acquired from Feige Brothers Company, a Saginaw manufacturer. All of it was sumptuously inlaid with different colored woods, accented with ebonizing, and french polished with layers of rubbed shellac. A label discovered on the hat rack indicates that it was made by a New York cabinetmaker named J. White, and in truth everything but the upholstered chairs was more in the vein of the elaborate furniture then produced in New York cabinet shops than of that from Michigan's factories. The parlor, used for the governor's receptions, was one of the most popular rooms in the building. Within a few years an upright piano would be added to the suite.

Senate chamber, circa 1900

House chamber, circa 1900

Supreme Court chamber, circa 1879

*All: State Archives of Michigan*

Those who enter the capitol through its main halls are drawn directly to the soaring rotunda, the heart of the building. Standing in the center of the glass floor, visitors look straight up at the starry oculus, or eye, of the interior dome far overhead.

*Photo by Balthazar Korab*



With the dedication, O. A. Jenison pasted his last clipping in the sixth volume of his scrapbooks. Not again until the present would any record of the capitol be so systematic, and his books survive as the principal source of information about the building's construction in the seven years following 1871. Old photographs in the State Archives of Michigan, taken through succeeding decades, show the capitol in a cavalcade of continuing change in Lansing. In the late 1870s Lansing was a town of wooden and some brick houses, few of either more than two stories high, except for one, which outshone them all, a mansion of dressed stone in part inspired by the new capitol. Workmen had been lured from the capitol to build "Barnes's Castle." This Gothic pile was the finest dwelling in town, but the capitol has outlived it. Through the 1880s and 1890s the avenues east of the capitol gradually filled with stores, hotels, and office buildings. Pavement replaced dirt and gravel in the streets, and sidewalks appeared, sometimes bordered by trees.

In the late nineteenth century the capitol readily became a center of activity and incident, along with its everyday use as public offices and a house of legislative assembly. Allan S. Shattuck, a house painter and war veteran, an ambitious man who did his painting with the use of only one arm, had a contract to paint the capitol dome, but found that no workman, including himself, was willing to climb to the pinnacle with bucket and brushes. Shattuck was an outspoken supporter of James A. Garfield for president of the United States in the election of 1880. During this especially heated election, he vowed that if Garfield won he would climb to the top of the capitol and fly the American flag. On Garfield's election, Shattuck's friends pressed for their reward. "That's the worst part of a man bragging," said Shattuck. But he made his climb, going out a lantern window, hugging the curving metal hulk of the structure, grabbing the spike on top, scrambling to the ball. The flag unfurled in the breeze and he could hear cheering from below. While aloft, he rigged a tackle as high as he could—probably on the finial—to facilitate the painting of the dome, and then he inched down.

Such an immense building, larger by far than any other around, was a natural attraction to children, and before the state took the matter under control, the capitol was a favorite after-school and weekend playground. Children ran in the hallways and up and down the stairs. "Both boys and girls slide astraddle down the handrails of the stairs," reported a newspaper. The building was open to the public every day with one, sometimes two guards on duty, hardly enough to stave the flow of children. This situation came to a tragic conclusion in the winter of 1881 when Bert Clippenger, a thirteen-year-old messenger for the House of Representatives, fell down a stairwell to his death while playing with friends. A general outcry closed the marble halls to play.

Boys and young men worked as pages in both chambers of the legislature, carrying messages and running errands. Seen here are the pages for the House of Representatives.

*State Archives of Michigan*

In 1907 President Theodore Roosevelt visited Lansing for the fiftieth anniversary celebration of Michigan Agricultural College. Driven in a locally manufactured REO automobile by its maker, R. E. Olds, the bombastic Roosevelt—who preferred horses to motorcars—appeared before the legislature in the capitol, the first president to do so, then agreed to go to the second-story porch outside the governor's office and address a large crowd that trampled the newly planted grounds in a delirium over the president's performance. That was in May; in September a constitutional convention was called to order at the capitol. Its work went fast and efficiently, and a new constitution was presented to the people and approved on November 3, 1908, the day of the national election in which William Howard Taft was elected Roosevelt's successor as president of the United States.

The capitol was dressed in finery for the visit of President Theodore Roosevelt on May 31, 1907.

*State Archives of Michigan*

The auditor general's office, circa 1900. The room was lit by gas, supplied by gas lines running overhead and fed to fixtures with open flames.

*State Archives of Michigan*

The adjutant general, who represented the military and veterans in the capitol, had an office prominently located on the first floor adjacent to the military museum; below it on the ground floor was the armory with its relics. By 1909, when half a century had passed since the Civil War, the importance of the adjutant general had diminished. Since space symbolizes power (and means power in fact) in any capitol, the auditor general began to look hungrily at this quiet, expansive territory of the adjutant general. A space war ensued that rose to bitter proportions, as the auditor general attempted to move the adjutant general out. Ultimately the auditor general won and the adjutant general left; but there was a compromise: the historic flags were not to leave the building. This beloved assemblage now included not only the Civil War battle flags but those from the Spanish-American War as well. The solution was reached of placing them on permanent display in the glass-floored rotunda. Accordingly eight marbleized bronze cases were purchased by bid and the flags installed there in 1910.

It would appear that the first interior decorator to work in the capitol who was not a decorative painter was Caroline Weber of Detroit, who made alterations in decorations and furnishings in 1909. She had worked on upholstery and furniture in the governor's office in 1878, but now her decorating was more extensive. Her ideas of good taste conflicted with the Victorian splendors of the capitol. She ordered many of the lesser gas fixtures removed and replaced with "electroliers," as electric ceiling fixtures were called. Furniture was sent out to be reupholstered. Carpeting in the legislative chambers was changed. Battleship linoleum was put over the wood floors of the basement corridors and in some of the offices adjacent.

When the government moved to the capitol, the building was too big. By the eve of World War I it was beginning to ache from overcrowdedness. A proposal in 1903 for a new state office building had come to nothing. Space wars were waged between departments. The adjutant general's battle was only the most conspicuous. Others fought as hard, as new departments moved in. At last, on May 10, 1917, the legislature passed an act to build a state office building in Lansing, to absorb a government growing larger every year. What was to be the Lewis Cass Building was under way after the war. In 1921, the year Eva McCall Hamilton, the first woman legislator of Michigan, reported for duty, the structure was boarded up and abandoned for lack of money and not completed until 1922.

SPACE WARS WERE WAGED BETWEEN DEPARTMENTS.
THE ADJUTANT GENERAL'S BATTLE WAS ONLY
THE MOST CONSPICUOUS.

AN IDEAL OF THE TIME
WAS THE CITY BEAUTIFUL,
A PLANNED URBAN SCENE
WORKED OUT
IN EVERY DETAIL.

The military museum and many offices moved to the new building, but the structure was only a partial solution. Where the government of another time had grown gradually too big for the capitol, postwar Michigan's government was growing so fast as to have a voracious appetite for new space. The capitol, unmistakably Victorian, had survived unscathed through an era in which many states built so-called Beaux-Arts capitols, whose architecture imitated academic Renaissance classicism. Examples are the new capitols built in Rhode Island, Minnesota, and Wisconsin. Though not copies of anything, they suggested the monuments of seventeenth- and eighteenth-century France and were decorated in a palatial manner.

The Michigan capitol was perhaps more acceptable than most Victorian buildings to the new classicism: Myers had given the facades a touch of academicism in his execution of pilasters and use of ashlar. Inside, the capitol bore the indelible brand of its own flamboyant age. By the 1890s such architecture was seen as the unhappy product of an era of excess. But as far as a state's citizens are concerned, a capitol need not be in style; it is loved for what it is and what it represents. Michiganians were proud of their capitol.

Its surroundings, however, were another matter. Lansing had not by any means grown older gracefully. And the matter of new annex buildings like the Cass Building: There would be more, and how would they be placed? Like the buildings on a university campus? Like the buildings of a downtown?

Late nineteenth- and early twentieth-century neoclassicism had developed as a by-product of its architectural renaissance an interest in city planning. An ideal of the time was the City Beautiful, a planned urban scene worked out in every detail. No greater model for this existed than the World's Columbian Exposition of 1893 in Chicago, a short-lived confection in plaster, water, landscape, and electric light. Planners were further inspired by the great success of the McMillan Plan for a revised Washington, D.C., made under the patronage of United States Senator James McMillan of Detroit. It was the blueprint for the ceremonial Washington we know today—the Mall and its flanking neoclassical buildings. Rare was the state capital city for the two decades after 1900 that did not have such a plan made for it. We see material evidence of this movement in Denver, where a well-considered plan was actually built in part, incorporating a capitol designed by Elijah Myers, and in Olympia, Washington. Archives over the country hold drawings for others, dreams never realized.

The Colorado State Capitol, finally completed in 1908, was also designed by Elijah Myers. Myers designed more state capitols than any other architect.

*Colorado Department of Public Relations*

A rally celebrating Michigan Agricultural College's victory over Ohio State University. The final score of the football game is inscribed on the photograph itself: M.A.C. 35, O.S.U. 20

*Michigan State University and Historical Collections*

ELIJAH MYERS'S CAPITOL WAS NO ALOOF MONUMENT.

So it was with Lansing. After World War I, concern was expressed increasingly about the appearance of the town and the crowded conditions in the state offices. In 1921 Harland Bartholomew, a Saint Louis city planner, produced a concept for a master plan for the capitol area that stretched from the head of Michigan Avenue to take over many blocks of the residential areas and vacant lots west of Capitol Square. Initially he suggested that the capitol be replaced eventually with a new building, and the bird's-eye view of his scheme shows a neoclassical capitol building in the World's Fair mode; this he changed, and he became very circumspect about saying anything against the capitol. Other new structures—to be built first—in this same white marble mode were distributed along tree-shaded axes and radial streets reminiscent of Washington, D.C. Reflector pools and parks enhanced the garden-like plan. Bartholomew encouraged the state to acquire all the property it could along the Grand River to turn into parkland.

Like most of the capitol schemes of the City Beautiful movement, this one proposed the virtual separation of the work places of lawmakers and state officials from town life. That had been the idea in Washington. It was the direct antithesis of the tradition that had prevailed in Lansing. Elijah Myers's capitol was no aloof monument. Big and extravagant as the age that created it, the capitol was part of the town; it was the symbol of the state and of Lansing. People passed through the capitol all day. Children had played there. School groups toured it, and their choirs performed, the boys and girls looking in wonder at the great chandeliers with their elk ornaments, marveling at the glass floor in the rotunda. Legislators walked from their offices out into the town, meeting to do business over drinks at the Olds Hotel across the street, or in any number of restaurants.

Bartholomew's plan would have made a major alteration to capitol life. It was an interesting idea on paper that was not to be. Michigan's capitol had grown up in a small town and had become part of it. Time would show that ideal plans imposed on this longtime friendship would come to nothing. Bartholomew returned to Lansing in 1938 with an improved master plan for a new capitol complex, with a new capitol and a governor's mansion. By that time many government offices had spilled beyond Capitol Square into state structures and rented space. The new plan caused a brief flare, then died down in that decade of the Great Depression, when the ideals of the City Beautiful seemed ever more distant and faint. It would not be until the era of historic preservation that the question of how things must go would be resolved.

The old Supreme Court chamber, now restored as a hearing room for the Senate Appropriations Commitee, 1993

*Photo by Balthazar Korab*

The 1930s closed with a state government grown much larger for the administrative load of the Depression. While the capitol had not ceased to serve its role, it was not held in the same reverence it had known, or so it seemed. Maintenance was more in the character of patching than repair. Alterations were made in a temporary way, with a point of view that seemed to assume that the old building was doomed. Three months before Pearl Harbor, Governor Murray D. Van Wagoner ordered removed from the glass cases in the rotunda thirteen captured southern Civil War flags and ceremoniously returned them to their native states. It was a magnanimous gesture, in a time when those who had been enemies in another century would soon join in the fiercest war in history.

During the war the building underwent some changes. One was "overflooring" of a few rooms, which had been carried out first in 1922 in the partial subdivision of the former state library, a tall interior on the west side of the building. This solution found space in the twenty-foot ceilings of the capitol by means of the horizontal subdivision of a single space into two floors connected by stairs. On the exterior, an attempt to clean the walls with sandblasting in 1944 caused such damage to the test spots that the project was abandoned. It was just as well. Some people thought cleaning a bad idea. Said Kenneth C. Black, a Lansing architect, "The Capitol building is an antique. Like all antiques, it immediately becomes subject to personal prejudices insofar as cleanliness is concerned. Cleaning is not advisable from an aesthetic point of view." So it could not be said that public opinion had grown apathetic on the subject of the capitol.

On Victory in Europe Day in May 1945 there was little open celebration in Lansing. That night the lights of the capitol dome, which had been dark since 1941, were turned on. When the Japanese surrendered in August, however, the town flooded with merrymakers. College student danced with factory worker. The Oldsmobile shift whistle blew into the night and the church bells rang. At dusk sunshine broke through the clouds. Wrote the *Lansing Journal*, "it was beautifully symbolic of peace." As for the capitol, peace meant the resumption of adjustments for more space. There was more overflooring. Machinery broke down and was replaced. The master clock, failed, was taken to the basement. Elevators for the House and Senate were put behind the chambers in the abandoned chimneys that had served the steam heating system.

Governor Fred W. Green with the governor's radio-equipped La Salle, circa 1930

*State Archives of Michigan*

EXIT
EXIT

The restored Senate chamber, 1990

*Photo by Dietrich Floeter*

# RESTORATION

In his message of January 1982, Governor William G. Milliken, who had heretofore supported the effort to replace the capitol, announced that he would appoint a committee "to study the condition of the building and make recommendations for its improvement and partial restoration." Personally he did not like the plan for a new capitol complex. He set his eye on the Michigan sesquicentennial of 1987, when he hoped the capitol, worn from use and brimming with offices and overfloors, would be spruced up. His committee recommended restoration. It was a period of recession; the governor knew he could put the expensive new capitol plan aside with little other explanation and leave restoration—if it was to be—to the future. A far larger project resulted. Rather than happening all at once, the movement to restore the capitol rolled slowly, but constantly, to the fore. Governor Milliken's committee decided to reorganize as the Friends of the Capitol and promote the idea.

The first work of restoration was the lobby outside the Senate chamber. William Kandler, secretary of the Senate, had urged that the area, which had become seedy from use, be restored properly, rather than simply redecorated. "Decorating costs money," he said, "and it has to be done over again when it goes out of style." A technical study was ordered of the original decorative painting of the lobby; lighting fixtures were restored, and necessary tables and chairs were built, copying originals left over from Elijah Myers's time. The result was so striking and seemed so correct for the building that for the first time in many years adjectives such as "wonderful" and "beautiful" were applied to the interior. The lobby project, though small compared to the great project, yet unplanned, that lay ahead, served as a promotion for the further restoration of the building. Kandler was clear in his intention, saying he hoped the Senate lobby was a "sparkplug to restoring the entire Capitol." Richard C. Frank, who in the 1960s had written the report for the committee of architects recommending the preservation of the building, advised Kandler on the lobby, and would return to serve as architect of the entire restoration.

An interest in restoration among some legislators led to a general discussion about the capitol. The next step, it was decided, might best be a master plan for preserving the old building that could be held up for comparison alongside the existing proposal for a new capitol in a larger complex. In July 1985 the legislature passed an act appropriating funds for a preservation master plan. A year later, on June 18, 1986, after interviewing others as well, the state selected Richard Frank to make the master plan for the capitol.

RATHER THAN HAPPENING ALL AT ONCE, THE MOVEMENT TO RESTORE THE CAPITOL ROLLED SLOWLY, BUT CONSTANTLY, TO THE FORE.

Governor William Milliken

*State Archives of Michigan*

THE MASTER PLAN URGED THAT THE BUILDING REMAIN FUNCTIONALLY ALIVE AND NOT BE RELEGATED TO MUSEUM STATUS.

A native of Louisville, Kentucky, Richard Calhoun Frank, at that time in his early fifties, had lived most of his life in Michigan, having offices at various times in Lansing and Detroit, as well as a branch office in Washington, D.C. He received his degree in architecture from the University of Michigan in 1953. Early on he developed a strong interest in historic preservation and restoration. When he developed the master plan, he was one of the best-known restoration architects in the United States. His projects numbered in the hundreds, covering thirty-six states, and included work on such monuments as the Library of Congress and such historical sites as Fort Michilimackinac in Michigan's northern Lower Peninsula. Aware that the plan needed to be a sales piece as well as a traditional master plan, he made his report a combination of fascinating discoveries, rich descriptions, and proposals for how to do the job.

"The master plan," he later wrote, "proved that the building could be returned to full functional efficiency and once again be the focal point of state government. It also demonstrated that this could be done within the building's original spaces, completely restored. The master plan urged that the building remain functionally alive and not be relegated to museum status." A team of twelve expert advisors in various fields worked with Frank on the plan during 1986-1987. The document outlined for the first time the possibilities for reusing the building within the standards of preservation principles. It was as much, and more significantly, a philosophical statement as an outline of physical work on the building. Frank recalled later on, "The primary planning challenge was to create a functional plan that was effective and yet would allow restoration of the building's original architectural character."

His concept was to make the capitol the "leadership meeting place" and to relocate the other functions in other buildings. All overflooring was to be removed, and the original 1870s spaces were to be restored with every modern convenience. Offices for the governor and lieutenant governor were to be in the offices "originally designed for them." He found that the first floor "could adequately house the entire leadership of the Senate and House of Representatives." The legislative chambers could be restored and continue in use as they had for a century, with "primary staffs" located nearby. In addition, "major committee rooms could be created in restored or rehabilitated space with connecting offices for the committee chairs." The challenge, wrote Frank in 1993, was that "if this functional solution was to work effectively into the next century, mechanical, electrical and communication systems, as well as life safety systems would have to be the same as for a completely new building."

"THE PRIMARY PLANNING CHALLENGE WAS TO CREATE A FUNCTIONAL PLAN THAT WAS EFFECTIVE AND YET WOULD ALLOW RESTORATION OF THE BUILDING'S ORIGINAL ARCHITECTURAL CHARACTER."

On February 11, 1987, leadership in the Senate announced plans for the restoration of the capitol. The project was to be supervised by the Michigan Capitol Committee, which would approve each step of the work. Senator John Engler, Senate majority leader, in joining Senator William Sederburg for the public statement, observed that in the past there had not been sufficient rules to protect the building. The committee was organized with the restoration in mind. Its power combined the forces of the House, the Senate, and the governor's office. Those who played the key roles in its creation—Engler, Sederburg, Speaker of the House Lewis Dodak, and Representative Richard A. Young, facilities officer for the House—built a strong committee that took an intimate role in decision making from the outset to the end of the project.

In May followed the completed preservation master plan, recommending a full-scale restoration and adaptation so that the building could continue in use as a state capitol. Proposed also was a plan for underground offices which was eventually dropped in preference for office buildings above ground. Over the summer of 1987 Frank supervised the restoration of the fourth-floor hearing and conference rooms used by the Senate and the House. "We were experimenting," he later said. "We learned a lot about the old building." Closed-up arches were reopened into the rotunda, skylights restored, and dropped ceilings removed. The House portion, which had been merely the upper part of the old library, finished in an essentially contemporary manner, while the Senate's rooms, intact, though in a part of the building left unfinished in the 1870s, were considered original spaces and given a historical treatment. The latter provided yet a second pilot showing what the building could be if restored.

The preservation master plan, meanwhile, was much in the newspapers, generating debate over the capitol and what should be done with it. Today it is clear from the stacks of clippings that the capitol had already been saved; the question was merely how it would be restored. Senator Engler took the lead in supporting the historical approach to restoration. From the House, Representative Dodak was a forceful voice in support of a major restoration, advocating a comprehensive approach. Senator Sederburg estimated that the project would cost $65 million and called it a "worthwhile investment." (The ultimate cost would fall considerably below his estimate at $58,117,746.91.)

The House chamber was still reasonably intact in 1906 (top), with light fixtures on the rostrum and hanging from the gallery. By 1985 (bottom) the walls had been covered with white acoustical tiles, tall glass screens had been installed in the gallery, and most of the original light fixtures had disappeared.

*Top: State Archives of Michigan*
*Bottom: Michigan Capitol Committee*

Frank proposed that the work be done in stages, or segments. The three major divisions would be the House, Senate, and executive spaces. The segments included the Senate chamber and adjacent spaces, the House chamber and adjacent spaces, the governor's office, the rotunda and the great corridors, the House and Senate offices, the ground-floor halls, and the exterior (the stonework, roof, and dome). To the committee, breaking up the work in this manner promised greater competitiveness in bidding and variety in talent, more direct control over the quality of the work, and flexibility in applying the lessons of one phase to the work of the next.

It was, moreover, significant to the committee that the capitol, the symbol of the state, not be closed entirely at any one time. The work segments were to dislocate as few as possible at a time and not to obstruct business. Some employees who moved from the building would return when the work on their areas was complete; others would be situated permanently in new offices nearby. Meanwhile school tours, performances in the rotunda, and heavy public visitation would continue along with the daily conduct of business, only at times necessarily diverted from the path of the work.

For each segment Frank was to provide a preservation analysis. "Implementing architects," selected through competition for individual segments, were to follow Frank's analysis and his continuing consultation. Frank himself was the architect for the Senate chamber and adjacent spaces. Implementing architects for the remainder of the Senate work were Architects Four of Ann Arbor; for the House, the corridors,and the rotunda, Wigen, Tincknell, Meyer & Associates of Saginaw; for the governor's suite and the exterior, Quinn Evans/Architects of Ann Arbor and Washington, D.C. The implementing architects, each chosen for particular skills, were able to concentrate on their sections of the monumental building while interacting with the other architects, state officials, and consultants in special fields, with greater results to the whole. The success of this unique approach provides a model for other capitol restorations.

The Senate chamber in 1906 (top) and just before restoration (bottom). In both chambers, the carpets were changed to a pattern featuring the state coat of arms and desks were rearranged in straight rows. In the Senate, walls were repainted a dark, murky green.

*Top: State Archives of Michigan*
*Bottom: Photo by Gregory Domagalski*

The Michigan Capitol Committee employed the Christman Company, a Lansing construction management firm, as project manager. Ronald D. Staley, head of the project for Christman, had his office in a group of connected trailers pulled up near the building's southwest side, and from there supervised the intricacies of scheduling, budget, bidding, and contracting and provided construction oversight and quality control. Jerry Lawler, appointed executive director of the Michigan Capitol Committee in March 1989, was a familiar presence in the trailer. It was his job to bring together the disparate elements of the project, to monitor the budget and schedule, and to settle disputes that naturally arose from time to time over different aspects of the work. A great part of his responsibility was to manage human relations. His was an especially critical role, for he was responsible not only for coordination, but also for keeping an interested committee informed of the progress of the work and for bringing before them issues that required their discussion and decisions.

THE SUCCESS OF THIS UNIQUE APPROACH PROVIDES A MODEL FOR OTHER CAPITOL RESTORATIONS.

To those who worked on the project, the meetings in the construction trailer's conference room hold a special place in memory. Busy, sometimes tense, at times intense, ever stimulating, the sessions in the crowded room with vinyl walls included, at their most populated, twenty or so in attendance, with Frank, Staley, and Lawler predictably there. From the outset John Beutler of the Senate staff and Tim Bowlin of the House staff were active participants in most of the deliberations and strong workers behind the scenes. Marty Selfridge of the Senate staff, who knew the building best because of his supervision of its ongoing maintenance, contributed immeasurably to simplifying complexities. Discussions might be on any construction or design subject, but the most complicated were usually over some matter of how to make a modern intervention compatible with the historic building, for that was a constant challenge and a subject never dropped from central focus.

The restored House chamber, 1990

*Photo by Balthazar Korab*

The restoration got under way late in 1988 with the Senate. Work on the House commenced soon after. The central part of the building, with corridors and rotunda, followed, with the governor's rooms next. While these projects were under way and some were completed, work began on the stone exterior, the restoration of the dome, and the building of a new copper roof. Meeting regularly in Senate rooms on the fourth floor in the capitol, the Michigan Capitol Committee kept close watch over the project, pushing it on to new segments, reviewing restoration procedures, and, essential to any public building project, seeing to its politics. Representative Richard Young was the first chairman of the committee, from late 1988 until early 1989, followed in the chairmanship by Senator Sederburg for the balance of 1989 and 1990. Senator John J. H. Schwarz, M.D., took office in 1991.

The restoration philosophy, as stated in the master plan, was firmly footed in the preservation of original materials wherever possible and the restoration of architectural features that had been altered. In application the lines were sometimes blurred. A mandate of the legislature was that the building function as a modern capitol. A revival of its historical appearance was to be the motif of the work, but the building had to serve and survive hard daily use.

THE RESTORATION PHILOSOPHY... WAS FIRMLY FOOTED IN THE PRESERVATION OF ORIGINAL MATERIALS WHEREVER POSSIBLE AND THE RESTORATION OF ARCHITECTURAL FEATURES THAT HAD BEEN ALTERED.

In many offices, restoration involved removal not only of overfloors but also of plaster, millwork, wiring, and heating ducts, down to bearing walls and brick arch subfloors.

*Photo by Thomas Gennara*

Because changes had to be made, it was decided to take a loyal approach to what was authentic to the period. Especially was this true of fixtures and furnishings. In many restorations of the time, as much was restored as could be, then modern elements were substituted for what was not known. This solution had not been successful in other places; indeed the results were usually confusing, the modern parts seeming in conflict with what was historic. Instead, it seemed that the building should envelop one visually in the period of its greatest vitality, the years from the 1870s to the completion of the highly elaborate painted wall and ceiling decorations in about 1890. In other words, the rooms should be finished and furnished in the style of Elijah Myers's original capitol.

“LET’S MAKE FACT OUR BASIS WHERE WE CAN,” HE SAID, “NOT GUESSWORK, FOR THAT COULD BE ANYBODY’S TASTE.”

Typical working offices in the restored capitol
*Photo by Dietrich Floeter*

Making the interiors harmonize with the architecture of the building had its perils, for it involved new design work in the old mode, the adjusting of historic models to suit modern needs. But the promise of harmony was the main selling point. The author of this volume was in charge of this aspect of the project, in cooperation with almost the entire balance of the restoration staff.

The building was to have much more furniture when restored than it had ever contained in its early years, but the idea of imposing contemporary office furnishings on the restoration was rejected from the start. A particularly successful solution to the need for hundreds of chairs was to select historic chairs that had been used in the capitol in the nineteenth century and make them models for “generic” chairs reproduced in great numbers and used throughout the building. Existing capitol furnishings were sought out and returned; some antique furnishings of the period were acquired; and numerous pieces were built in the Senate carpentry shop that followed Elijah Myers’s simpler preferences or were designed anew for modern purposes in the “reform” or vernacular style of his time.

Whenever anything was introduced that had no source in the original building, the question recurred, “How to make it blend in a Victorian way?” All parties labored over this issue again and again, and the successful results are one of the prime assets of the capitol’s rebirth. The question was put not only to furniture, but to everything else about the restoration that would be visible—hardware, lighting, woodwork, flooring, and innumerable fancy paint treatments.

By the time the work began in 1988 the approach centered entirely in the historic building; underground offices had been omitted from the plan as prohibitively expensive (although at about the same time Texas approved that concept for its capitol, another Myers building). Michigan’s capitol temporarily emptied space by space, the employees and elected officials scattering to various state office structures and notably, after late 1990, to the Olds Hotel across the street, which was remodeled for state offices.

With the first hammer and crowbar came the test of the master plan. In a restoration, more than in new construction, one decision may affect many others. Research on the building never stops, for new information is likely to present itself as the structure is pierced and opened up. This may be a large-scale, worthwhile discovery, such as the outline of a door long-covered; or it may be whimsically small—and of little value to posterity—like the whiskey bottle found tucked away between Senate walls.

A doorway, walled up and forgotten, was rediscovered during restoration when wall coverings were removed.
*Photo by Thomas Gennara*

Senate chamber during the demolition phase of the restoration. Senators held session temporarily in the old Supreme Court chamber.

*Photo by Alan Kamuda*

Richard Frank, realizing that his work must set an example for the rest, took personal charge as architect of the first phase, the Senate wing, on the building's south side, which contained the Senate chamber and offices. It was learned very quickly that to restore may mean to demolish first. Most of the original plaster was found either exposed or buried under later walling. Severe damage caused by a 1970 overflooring, together with long years of dry artificial heat, made it necessary to consider and at last adopt a plan for new plaster in many places. In making this decision, Frank observed that it was the admission of overflooring that had saved the building from demolition, and that the replacement of the plaster was a small concession. The secretary of the Senate, Dr. Willis Snow, who represented the Senate in day-to-day decisions on the work, was particularly interested, however, that the new work be as authentic as possible, even though the concept of use had been greatly expanded. "Let's make fact our basis where we can," he said, "not guesswork, for that could be anybody's taste." (It was a tall order in a building so exposed to hard use for over a century, but it became almost a motto and was to influence an adherence, at least in tone, in all parts of the capitol's restoration.)

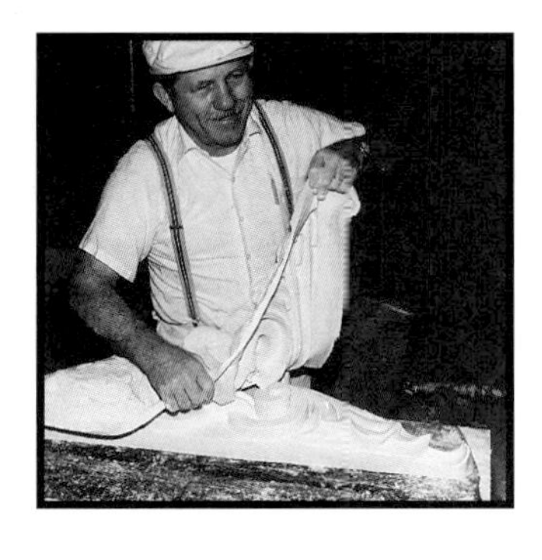

A latex mold is used to cast missing window and door ornaments, which were originally painted to look like wood (top). Custom templates were crafted to recreate missing cornices (bottom).

*Top: Photo by Gregory Domagalski*
*Bottom: Photo by Thomas Gennara*

Ultimately much of the 1870s plaster was saved. Almost all of that in the corridors and the House and Senate chamber and adjacent areas is original, pointed up and refreshed.

With the plaster came the problem of the decorative painting. Earliest photographs show the walls of Michigan's capitol stark white, as they were left unpainted for six years after the dedication, partly to allow the plaster to season. The legislature appropriated $25,000 in June 1885 to decorate the Senate and House chambers, the Supreme Court chamber, the governor's parlor, the front corridor, and the rotunda. So pleased were the lawmakers with the results that another $20,000 was voted two years later to the month. At last, in 1889, a decade after

In the 1870s plaster strengthened with horsehair was used to finish walls and ceilings in the capitol as well as for pilasters and elaborate cornices. This early photograph of the entrance corridor shows still-unpainted white walls.

*State Archives of Michigan*

the building was dedicated, they approved a final $10,000 to finish the work. Peeled walls, old photographs, and surviving ornamental painting confirmed that the original decorations had been very ambitious.

The mandate of the master plan was to make the research complete before attempting new work. Before the plaster was touched, Darla M. Olson of New York, a conservator and one of the nation's leading scholars of decorative painting, made a thorough investigation of the original colors and designs that had been on the ceilings and walls. Some of the decorative paintings were buried under as many as twenty layers of plain paint, while the numerous decorative ensembles that remained had been overpainted in an effort to refresh them. Darla Olson's initial work was that of the conservator and archivist, rescuing the information. Like archaeologists, she and her crew painstakingly peeled back layers of obscuring paint and overpaint to gain an overall picture.

Most of her work, however, was recording. When the original painting program was completed, the building had nine acres of decorative painting—an odd way to describe it, perhaps, but suggestive of the scale of conservation and restoration involved. She transferred the designs, full scale, to large Mylar sheets. The colors were examined beneath microscopes to determine their original hues, allowing for the accumulation of dirt and grime and for special effects made with shellac and varnish glazes.

## Decorative Paint Research and Restoration

1

First, a chemical stripper is brushed onto the wall to soften initial layers of paint. The researcher must strip an area broad enough to reveal the design buried beneath layers of plain wall paint.

2

Second, the worker carefully scrapes away the softened paint. Only a few layers are removed at a time. This process is repeated over and over, taking care not to destroy the layer beneath.

3

Third, original colors and designs, in this case a brilliant federal shield and swag design, emerge from the softened overpaint.

4

Fourth, once the entire design has been revealed, a clear sheet of Mylar is placed over it.

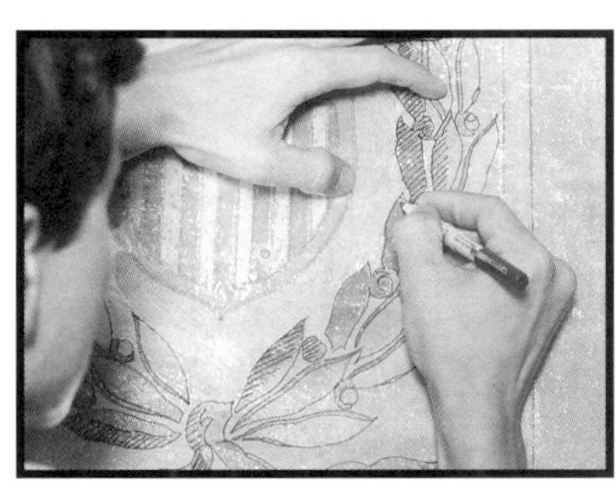

5

Fifth, the design is meticulously traced onto Mylar. Paint color samples are taken in each area of the design. These are studied under the microscope and analyzed to determine original colors and finishes, and then keyed into the design.

6

Sixth, following the information recorded by the paint researcher and using stencils enhanced by freehand work, highly skilled decorative painters recreate the original pattern in authentic colors, using modern paints.

*Numbers 1–5: Photos by Thomas Gennara*
*Number 6: The Christman Company*

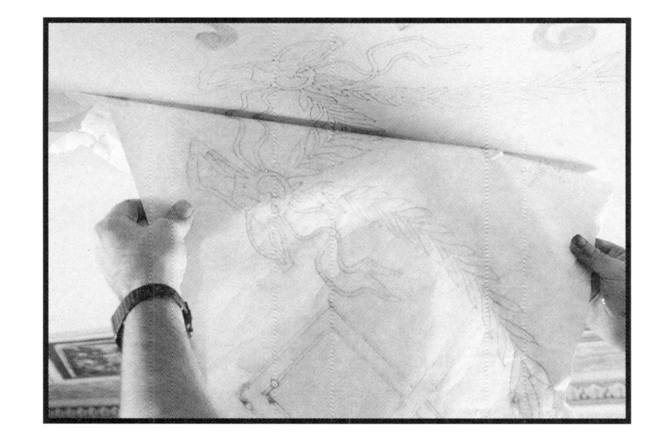

Transferring a ceiling design onto Mylar

*Photo by Thomas Gennara*

The second part of the work was writing specifications for restoration or reconstruction of the painted surfaces, for it had been determined to reproduce all that were missing and restore where possible all that survived. The primary paint contractors, Evergreene Painting Studios and John Canning & Co., substituted modern products for historic ones, for example, replacing bronze powder gilding with acrylic gold, which holds its color longer.

When the building materials such as plaster and wood were removed in different spaces as far as was intended, utilities—electrical wiring, air conditioning chillers, ducts, fire systems—were installed, usually trenched into the brick walls, now stripped of their plaster. Where original plaster was to survive, the trenches were kept as modest as possible with the idea that they would be repaired. Old flooring, which by 1988 represented quite a variety, was removed and replaced by thin raised flooring of concrete tiles set on a grid. These could be unbolted and lifted like trap doors to give access to utilities, with no overall disturbance to the room. Shaw-Winkler, Inc., F. D. Hayes Electric Company, and Quality Electric installed pipe and approximately 380 miles of cable beneath these tiles for the new systems in the capitol. Space was left for any new computer wiring which technology might dictate in the future.

Installation of the Senate chamber flooring. The floor was raised five inches to allow for additional electrical wiring and cabling.

*Michigan Capitol Committee*

Woodwork was saved wherever possible. Some had to be reproduced because the original was missing. It will be remembered that black walnut had been used in special spaces such as the major offices and elsewhere pine painted to resemble walnut had imitated it. In some rebuilt areas actual walnut was substituted for pine in the interest of saving on the future cost of maintenance. For the whole building 398 windows were reproduced, some in Scotland, others in Iowa and Detroit, as double-pane insulated versions that could not be told from the old. Mahogany was used in place of the original pine framing; paint graining was applied to make the wood resemble walnut. Grainers worked in the building for several years, building up from the base coat, applying pigment by hand to create the effect of natural walnut wood grain.

Tools of the decorative painter

*Photo by Thomas Gennara*

In general the areas adjacent to the Senate chamber, or the second and third floors just outside the chamber, were returned to the original plan, which had been much changed, particularly over the previous twenty-five years. Since a great number of the occupants of the building were permanently relocated in other buildings in the capitol area as part of realizing the concept of the capitol as a "leadership meeting place," there was need for fewer offices and more conference rooms. A by-product of this change was the availability of more public space and more general space for the legislative functions. The sense of crowdedness would be ended.

In the Senate chamber, a well-documented room, original objects were meticulously restored, notably the members' desks. New lecterns for speaker stations were designed to complement the desks and built in the carpentry shop. Many refinements were missing, for example, the original interior shutters and some of the lighting; but the principal chandeliers of crystal, glass, and metal did remain and required only refitting. Missing original lighting was reproduced. This included magnificent Gothic-style brass standard lamps for gas—now electrified—that had been lined up on the rostrum. The combination pendant fixtures for gas and electricity that had been added along the edges of the gallery were reproduced in high-polish brass, as they appeared in the old photographs of the chamber.

The chamber's fine portraits were cleaned, including that of General Lafayette, after one painted in 1824 by Ary Scheffer and presented by Lafayette to Congress in Washington. It had hung in all Michigan's capitols. The results of conservation of a nineteenth-century full-length portrait of Michigan's

## Wood Graining

1

2

3

4

5

6

Graining is the art of hand painting a surface to imitate wood. A variety of methods may be used in graining, depending on the wood being imitated. At the capitol these steps were generally followed:

- First, the surface is stripped of layers of overpaint and an oil-based coat applied. The color of this base coat depends on the wood being imitated, in this case, dark walnut.

- Second, deglossing with fuller's earth to prevent beading or "cissing" allows the application of the next coat, a mixture of dry pigment, water, and flat beer. (Beer acts as a binder.) A special brush with long, flexible bristles, called a flogger, is beaten lightly over the wet pigment, creating the appearance of pores in the wood. This is allowed to dry.

- Third, another oil-based coat is brushed on. This step, called "scumbling," adds a mixture of pigment, linseed oil, turpentine, and a drying agent to the surface. This coat is also lightly flogged to spread the pigment evenly, and allowed to set.

- Fourth, a special pointed brush is used to draw lines to imitate grain. Painted grain is applied to simulate the way a cabinetmaker uses natural grain: heart grain is imitated for door panels, for example; straight grain for stiles and rails.

- Fifth, "softened" by lightly brushing with a clean, dry brush, the lines are blended to achieve realism. Brushes called overgrainers are used to add detail.

- Finally, after drying, the surface is again deglossed and brushed with a beer-water-pigment mixture. It is now ready for "mottling," in which a special short-bristled handleless brush lifts and deposits pigment to create the shimmering ripples seen in wood. Two coats of varnish are applied to protect the graining.

*Numbers 1–2, 6: Michigan Capitol Committee*
*Numbers 3–5: Photos by Thomas Gennara*

Restored Senate chamber from the rostrum. At the rear is a portrait of Russell Alger, Civil War hero and governor, 1885–1886. Above, ruby and white glass panels in both chamber ceilings once again feature state coats of arms, replicating originals discarded decades before.

*Photo by Balthazar Korab*

famous statesman Lewis Cass proved more interesting than had been anticipated. It had been noticed that the figure, pose, and setting were very similar to those in Gilbert Stuart's 1797 portrait of George Washington, known as the "Lansdowne portrait," which hangs in the East Room of the White House. The Michigan legislature, while still sitting in Detroit in the 1830s, had appropriated $100 for a portrait of Washington, which the most intense effort has not been able to locate, even in the records. Copies of the Lansdowne portrait were very commonly seen in legislative halls of that time. When the Cass portrait was cleaned by the conservator Alfred Ackerman at the Detroit Institute of Arts, it was found that the head had been overpainted. Could the head have been substituted for that of Washington at some point, perhaps at the time of Cass's death in 1866? The portrait was cleaned as it was, leaving its mystery intact.

The use of computers at the members' desks had been discussed and was at last decided on. It was clear that the computer was the means by which lawmakers would connect with their offices in Lansing and at home, with the library, and in some cases with their constituents; moreover, computers would be used to trace legislation and call up statutes and administrative rules. There being no way of adapting the existing historic desks to this purpose, they were restored to their original varnish finish, and the functional office desk chairs of more recent years were reupholstered and put back into service. For the computers a completely separate side console was developed through the designs of architects Eugene Hopkins and Clark Andreae. This innovation solved many problems, providing space for a computer screen and keyboard, telephone, and storage, all of which could be covered up when not in use.

The color scheme used in the Senate chamber—largely blue and blue-green, with golds, dusty yellows, and some brown—followed the original. Carpeting was designed in an Oriental pattern, and it was gratifying to find at a later date, when a scrap of the original turned up in a chicken coop, that it was very close to what had been designed. Myers's tin ceiling, intact, was repainted as he had ordered originally; some of his fancy cartouches, painted on the walls, also survived and were conserved. Restored, the room looked remarkably as it must have when completed; electric voting boards receded into the original wall colors, while artificial lighting, falling through restored skylights of etched glass, supplemented the daylight of former times.

The offices off the corridors to the rear and above the chamber were simpler in their decorative design, but in their way equally rich. Their decor was recreated in minute detail. As their ceilings seemed to soar after the removal of the overflooring, the richness of the decorations took full flight. A new conference room was created on the southwest corner of the second floor. Two original office spaces were thrown together, and Darla Olson combined the original decorative schemes into one. The room was furnished with a twenty-foot-long table reused from an earlier Senate conference room and covered with green baize and with chairs reproduced from an original cane-back armchair found in the state archival collections that had served in the old Lansing capitol and in the new one as well. The addition of an antique pier mirror, deeply upholstered armchairs, and historic paintings borrowed from the Detroit Institute of Arts completed a striking interior, lighted by reproductions of original gas chandeliers from the capitol. In this room and the others of the Senate restoration, lace curtains were introduced with great success. Their practicality was seen immediately in their value as insulation. They diffused the light from outside, and their patterns gave special Victorian éclat.

The first phase of the Senate work was completed on January 10, 1990, with a large celebration. Six months before, on July 28, 1989, restoration had commenced in the House wing. Generally speaking, the philosophy that had governed the work in the Senate was applied to the House and resulted in many of the same solutions. As for the other segments of the restoration, Richard Frank remained the preservation architect here. Wigen, Tincknell, Meyer & Associates of Saginaw, represented by John T. Meyer, were implementing architects, with the consultants Frank had assembled for the first phase. The restoration team interacted with the office of the Speaker of the House, Lewis Dodak, particularly through Lindy Hover, chief of staff, and Tim Bowlin, the House business manager. Regular meetings were held to coordinate the work and review altered and new decisions necessitated by discoveries in the pulling apart of the House wing.

Called today the Elijah Myers Room, this committee room behind the Senate chamber was created from two original offices.

*Photo by Balthazar Korab*

House chamber during demolition. The chamber is the largest room in the capitol, measuring 100 by 70 feet with a 40-foot ceiling. Representatives held session temporarily in another building during this segment of the restoration.

*Michigan Capitol Committee*

House chamber during restoration. In both chambers, decorative painters and other restorers worked high above the floor on scaffolding.

*Photo by David A. Trumpie*

The restored House of Representatives chamber

*Photo by Dietrich Floeter*

The House chamber, although 30 percent larger, is almost an architectural duplicate of the Senate, with its skylight of etched glass, its rows of Renaissance Revival pilasters, and its gallery. Although the size of the House membership has grown by only ten since the building was built, the room is quite filled with its work. The desks, though rearranged at Richard Frank's insistence in the historic "fan" arrangement, literally touch side to side. Because of the cost, there are no computer consoles, but the restoration incorporated the wiring for them.

The restored room holds its large responsibility well. The shell was carefully brought back to its 1880s appearance. Its intensity seems to swallow the numerous contents, taking away any sense of crowdedness. Like the Senate it has a gala, opera-house quality, the color here being the original deep terra cotta, used with teal blue, among other colors, and various bronze, copper, and gilt effects. For the carpet, the previous mid-twentieth-century all-over pattern of Michigan state coat of arms was revised. The coat of arms was incorporated instead into a broad Victorian border, and the new central field, which, except for the central aisle, was largely obscured by furniture, was given a simple repeating motif of smaller scale. The historic lighting style of the House is identical to that in the Senate.

Michigan state coat of arms from the border of the House chamber carpet

*Michigan Capitol Committee*

Likewise, the arrangement of the House office section is similar to that of the Senate. Two conference rooms were created, one on the east and one on the west, where smaller rooms had been. Each seats some fifty around long tables. Historic portraits are hung here, with reproduction gas fixtures, elaborately patterned custom-made carpeting, and heavy window curtains.

More individual offices were included in this phase of the restoration than in the Senate phase, where only the lieutenant governor's capitol office, located on a corridor behind the Senate, was considered. There was much discussion over how these restored offices would work. Years had passed since the days of walnut desks and large cabinets. Office workers were accustomed to vinyl and gray metal, tweed-pattern carpeting, neutral walls, and bright fluorescent lighting. Moreover, the computer had made its appearance, transforming somewhat the character of the work space. Historical evidence of how the offices had looked was very sparse; one or two photographs showed corners of offices. Paint analysis revealed decorative wall and ceiling treatments, most of which had been covered up.

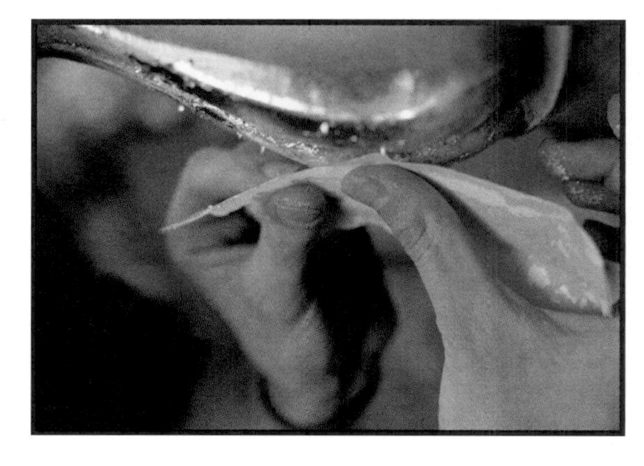

Gold leaf is applied in thin sheets. This and acrylic gold paint were used throughout the historical spaces.

*Photo by Thomas Gennara*

In designing modern offices the old way the rule applied with the greatest success was to provide abundant surface space and plenty of cabinets. These two elements seemed to outshine most other needs, for they had been necessarily denied in the makeover offices of the overfloor era and are seldom available in the average office of contemporary design. Wall-mounted cabinets, the upper shelves of some reached by ladders or steps, proved especially useful. A variation on the nineteenth-century wardrobe was another happy solution to space, for these provided coat closets, coffee stands, and storage; besides, they were large and even formidable pieces and tended to dominate and thus establish a design theme that overshadowed the necessary presence of computers, typewriters, and filing cabinets, many of which were office equipment from before the restoration. Made in walnut, the new furniture featured chamfered corners, incised decorations in various forms, and, for a surface finish, a deep gloss far removed from the popular satin texture generally used today. Most of the furnishings for the offices were made by the carpentry shops of the House and Senate. Their ability to meet this challenge is unique among state capitol restorations.

The restored east entrance corridor, with "gas" chandeliers and replication "collar" electric lights on the columns. The original collars were removed years ago.

*Photo by Dietrich Floeter*

Lighting was a particular challenge. Originally, it will be remembered, the building had been lighted by a combination of gas and natural light, the latter a major element because the capitol was to be used mostly in the daytime. (Today the building is likely to be in use at any time from six in the morning to midnight.) After the introduction of electricity the skylights seemed unnecessary, and once the building was air conditioned they were also considered unwanted sources of heat; so they were gradually covered over. From the start Richard Frank had wanted to reopen the skylights, to return to the building one of Elijah Myers's major architectural effects, the flow and ebb of natural light.

The original gas corridor chandeliers (top) were electrified around the turn of the century. In the 1960s, electric candles replaced glass globes (middle). Restored (bottom), they regain their original appearance.

*Top: State Archives of Michigan*
*Middle: Michigan Capitol Committee*
*Bottom: Photo by Dietrich Floeter*

The capitol's original gaslights, while in some cases very elaborate, were not as numerous as the reproduced ones in use there today. Historically the open flame of a gas burner was merely an improved, safer substitute for the candle or oil lamp flame. In the 1870s artificial light was still seen as a supplement to natural light, not a substitute for it. Electricity

HISTORIC FIXTURES WERE TO BE REPRODUCED OR RESTORED, AND WHERE THERE WAS NO INFORMATION ABOUT THE ORIGINALS, ONES APPROPRIATE TO THE PERIOD AND DESIGN WERE TO BE USED.

made the great change by disposing of the flame, and a never-ending appetite for the brighter, more general artificial illumination of electricity resulted in the high level of light we demand today. A by-product of modern electric illumination is the windowless room. Michigan's capitol has only one of these among its official spaces, a small meeting room made from a former storeroom near the Senate chamber.

The restoration rejected "down lights"—the recessed ceiling spotlights ubiquitous in contemporary buildings and unhappily present in many historic restorations—in the belief that they were inappropriate to the historic quality of the capitol. Historic fixtures were to be reproduced or restored, and where there was no information about the originals, ones appropriate to the period and design were to be used. Various ideas for supplementary lighting were tried but dropped in favor of equipping the reproduced gas fixtures with sufficient electric light, to be combined where necessary with task lighting, or desk lamps.

"Up lights" in the restored rotunda

*Photo by Balthazar Korab*

Some modern innovations were used in lighting the capitol. The most intrusive of these are "up lights" in the balcony floors of the rotunda, which "wash" the decorative paint and portraits with light on overcast days. Elsewhere strong lights concealed behind the etched-glass skylights of the chambers, when turned on, provide light as bright as day. The ceremonial spaces nearly all have television lighting. In the offices and most spaces, however, the reproduction gaslights, electrified, do the work. Several types were original, reproduced from photographs or from examples that had survived in the building. Many were designed after fixtures of the period, to give variety, and as a consideration for lower cost in manufacturing. Where a number of the offices may have had only wall brackets, all now have chandeliers, for the practical and more agreeable distribution of light from overhead.

The first episode of the House work ended with a celebration on April 24, 1990, in the restored House chamber. While two of the most significant parts of the work were completed, there was much more yet to go. The next phase had been under way since midsummer in the east and west corridors of the ground floor. (The north-south cross-corridors were a separate project undertaken in 1991.) Architects Four of Ann Arbor were selected as implementing architects, represented by Eugene Hopkins, who had consulted on the Senate chamber furniture for Richard Frank.

Attic over the Senate chamber before (left) and after (right) restoration. Original skylights have been uncovered and replaced so that natural light can pass through the glass ceiling into the chamber below. The area was also painted white to increase reflectivity.

*Michigan Capitol Committee*

The ground floor rotunda and corridors originally led only to the armory and store rooms, which quickly became offices. Today, this area is likely to be filled with schoolchildren on tour.

*Photos by Dietrich Floeter*

Traditionally the corridors were stepchildren of the capitol, their walls lined with storage closets, their original architecture defaced by quick and temporary solutions. It had been so from the beginning. Elijah Myers had wanted a slate floor in this space, but his thrifty commission intervened and ordered less expensive wood, which was later covered with linoleum. One of the first decisions of the restoration was to honor Myers's idea, but when slate proved too difficult to maintain, a substitute was made of a contemporary speckled, dark-gray tile that bears some similarity to it. Twentieth-century cabinets lining the halls were torn out. Metal-framed glass doors to the rooms were removed and the original arched door openings restored. Darla Olson's research yielded evidence that the plaster walls had been scored to suggest stone laid in ashlar, or rectangular, blocks. This effect was reproduced with great success. Without original hall lighting or evidence of it, reproductions were made of fixtures that appeared in an old postcard photograph of the armory, which had been located on this floor. These were rolled tin gaslights, double-branched, painted a very red terra cotta and banded with gilt. Hung in precise rows, they give a visual effect of duplication that makes them resemble reflections in facing mirrors, emphasizing the length and lowness of the corridors to great advantage.

The third major thrust of the restoration took place in the upper corridors and rotunda. Wigen, Tincknell, Meyer & Associates, represented by John Meyer, were appointed implementing architects. Richard Frank had long considered this one of the most significant parts of the capitol project because of the excellent state of preservation of the painted and ornamental plaster wall decorations of the corridors and the painted walls in the rotunda, an artwork program carried all the way up to a starry inner dome. "The dusty, dim paintings we see today," he said, "bear no relation to what we will see." He was concerned about how these might be given artificial light, and that decision was to be long in coming. Darla Olson began her investigation work on the decorative paint there in the summer of 1990 and was preparing specifications for restoration in the fall of 1991, when the actual structural work began.

Decorative painter restoring a detail under a gallery in the rotunda. Although many designs were restored using stencils, extensive freehand painting was necessary to regain original detailing and depth.

*Photo by Thomas Gennara*

The rotunda ringed by cases filled with replicas of Civil War battle flags

Photo by Dietrich Floeter

No single part of the building was so nearly untouched by alteration as the corridors and rotunda area, and thus no part was so carefully conserved. The grand hallways, with their checkerboard black and white Vermont marble flooring, had for generations delighted those with an appetite for the dramatic in architecture. The plaster decorations on the walls still had their deep color and textured effects. Painted ceilings still suggested courtyards in a Moorish palace, open to azure skies. And the chandeliers, those fantastic creations by the long-forgotten Mitchell, Vance & Company of New York, with the elk playing among the gas jets, survived and still thrilled.

Only one of the hallway's great chandeliers was missing, having crashed to the floor in the 1960s. The absent fixture was reproduced, and the nineteen surviving originals were restored, their historic finishes duplicated and their gas jets rewired once again for electricity. Other lighting was necessary. A dialogue ensued as to whether the new lighting should be a new element, movable torchères that stood on the floor, or whether it would be better to mount newly designed permanent fixtures, which had been typical in Elijah Myers's original scheme. Lighting consultant Gary Steffy from Ann Arbor showed ways in which both might work. Preservationists objected to fixing anything new to the walls, yet this was the ultimate solution. "Gas" brackets were designed along the idea of the type used in the building in the 1870s, clusters of gas globes held out from an elaborate cast cartouche.

The rotunda itself is relatively small in diameter for a capitol rotunda, but its human scale is a part of its charm. It still has its old greenish glass floors, through which light passes below, and its space rises beyond ring after ring of balconies to a play of daylight entering through the drum of the dome.

In this rotunda, like relics in a church, the cherished battle flags of the Civil War were lined up in glass cases. If the capitol when new could thank the Civil War flags in part for its very existence, then the flags could now thank the capitol for harboring them all these years. They showed their age more than the building, hanging, some of them, in tatters from their old, worn staffs. Now they were removed to the Michigan Historical Museum to be conserved, photographed, and studied, then to go into the highest level of protective storage, away from dust and light. They were to be displayed only on a rotating basis, but accessible under controlled conditions to scholars and the public. Experts busied themselves making copies, which would be returned to the rotunda to represent the originals.

Fragile Civil War battle flags being removed from the capitol during the restoration

Photo by David A. Trumpie

The inner dome with scaffolding

Photo by Thomas Gennara

The rotunda was filled with scaffolding, rising 150 feet and weighing 40 tons, for the repair and conservation of the decorative paint. And a compelling sight it was, the needle-like structure's ascent higher and higher into the fall of natural light. It was garlanded with strands of light bulbs for the convenience of working, and ladders and stairs simplified ascent and descent. The different plank floors provided platforms for the painters' supplies, including chemicals for cleaning and paints which they mixed on the site on palettes for inpainting. Smells of varnish signaled the completion of the project.

It turned out on investigation that the allegorical paintings in the dome had been painted elsewhere on canvas and applied directly to the curved metal walls with glue and nails. These allegories of eight female figures, representing Science, Art, Labor, Education, Law, Commerce, Industry, and Agriculture, were restored in place, eighty feet in the air, by conservators from the Detroit Institute of Arts.

Where the canvas had become detached from the wall it was reglued. Chipped or flaking paint was secured if possible and missing paint replaced by inpainting, but the major work was actually only cleaning and sealing, as the paintings were generally in good condition.

The rotunda's restoration was still under way when Architects Four began work as implementing architects on the old Supreme Court room on the third floor, immediately above the governor's office. Eugene Hopkins worked with the capitol consultants and the restoration team.

Conservator working on one of the rotunda allegorical paintings

Photo by Thomas Gennara

Photo by Thomas Gennara

Painted on eight-foot-high canvases and glued to the curved walls of the inner dome, allegorical figures represent institutions important to a young and growing state.

Photos by Dietrich Floeter

The old Supreme Court chamber, during restoration and after the work was completed. The ceiling is one of the few in the capitol which was never overpainted. It was cleaned and conserved in much the same manner as a work of fine art.

*Top: Photo by Thomas Gennara*
*Bottom: Photo by Balthazar Korab*

The room was a remarkable interior even in an unrestored state after more a century of use. Since 1970 it had served as the Senate Appropriations Room, a hearing room accessible to the public. The restoration was to respect the room's historic integrity while allowing it to work at its more recent task. Elijah Myers's decorative plasterwork survived, notably a frieze of simulated tiles in an Anglo-Japanese mode, reflecting a popular taste for Asian design in his time. In the decorative painting, done after his tenure as architect, poinsettias, created in relief, adorn the walls, and the ceiling motif is Pompeiian, representing the atrium of a Roman house.

Behind the judges' bench of black walnut rose a powerful and highly architectural screen of cabinets in the same material. These had been made originally by Feige Brothers Company of Saginaw. For the most part they needed only cleaning of a wax buildup and repolishing to restore their lustre and preserve the patina of age. Otherwise, the room had lost its fixtures and furnishings. These were to be replaced in part. The shell of the room was restored and its decorative painting conserved, the old colors and original mottled treatments reproduced where necessary. The bench and cabinets were retained. Hopkins designed desks arranged before these in a horseshoe, to seat the appropriations committee. In front of this was a small audience section, furnished with rows of chairs reproduced from those used earlier in the building. Since the room was to be used often for presentations by the public to the committee, Hopkins designed a special screen, which could be concealed mechanically when not in use, to allow the audience to view the same display the committee members would see on individual screens at their seats. Not built at this writing, it remains part of future plans.

The gas chandeliers that had once hung here but had been replaced were reproduced, and wall brackets were designed in the same mode to provide additional light. Light for television cameras was required here, as in many other spaces. This need is perhaps fleeting, for innovations in camera design make studio level lighting less and less a necessity on location. The solution was to use theater spotlights mounted along the upper walls on pipe bars such as pictures were hung from in Victorian times. Pipe bar and light were painted the predominant wall color. In this case, they would have destroyed original fabric if hidden, and unlike the chambers, this room had no skylights. The same plan was adopted for television lighting elsewhere in the building.

No interior in the Michigan capitol presents a more brilliant palette than the old Supreme Court. A carpet was designed in an 1870s style, based as far as possible on a dim sketch of the original, with an Anglo-Japanese flavor and rich coloration of blue and red. Rolling off the mill at U.S. Axminster in Greenville, Mississippi, it made a fearful sight, and many were the worries over this particular carpet, even though dozens of others had been designed for the capitol. When the carpet was laid it was perhaps in the one place on earth where it truly belonged, for it drew the disparate elements of the old Supreme Court room together as neatly as a package tied up in ribbon.

The state library as it appeared originally, about 1879 (bottom). It was overfloored in 1969 to create legislative offices. Overfloors were removed during restoration (middle). The House Appropriations Room (top) was created from the upper two floors. Unlike most spaces in the restored capitol, it takes its finishes and colors in walls and carpeting from a largely contemporary palette.

*Top: Photo by Balthazar Korab; middle: photo by Thomas Gennara*
*Bottom: State Archives of Michigan*

While the Supreme Court project took place a House Appropriations Room was built in part of the volume once occupied by the state library, a skylit space which had extended along the west front, three stories (from the second floor to the fourth), divided within only by galleried bookcase stacks. Heretofore the House Appropriations Committee had occupied a temporary addition to the building which Capitol Archivist Kerry Chartkoff described as a "carbuncle" of a structure. The fourth-floor level of the library space had been subdivided by overflooring in 1922, when the state library moved elsewhere, leaving only the law library. The latter moved at last in 1969, leaving the rest to be subdivided. Richard Frank did not recommend the restoration of the library space. The library already had its own building, and the capitol housed no function for which such a vast, open area was appropriate. He was willing to apply the preservation philosophy of adaptive reuse to this area, a concept very different from that underlying the rest of the work. Here the shell was preserved but put to a new and very different use.

The House Appropriations Room and the meeting spaces above it are thus the only contemporary spaces in the building, in terms of their treatment. Richard Frank had established the motif in the renovation of the fourth-floor conference rooms earlier in the decade, and John Meyer continued the idea in the House Appropriations Room. These rooms of the third and fourth floor, though embellished with some Victorian elements, stand out boldly alien in the context of the rest of the building. The spaces are essentially modern and very clearly remodeled. The past appears here in fragments of the old library, such as iron columns, that were left as found, and in reproduced windows. The contemporary idea is challenged by the use of historical pattern in furniture and carpeting, though the carpeting is rendered in contemporary colors. Large and elaborate chandeliers of the original period of the building have been reproduced for the room. Flag cases have been built to display the flags of current Michigan veterans' organizations.

The last of the ceremonial spaces to be restored was the governor's office, commenced in April 1991, after research and planning. This series of rooms had for all practical purposes virtually vanished in remodelings, but they had never been overfloored. Subdivided in other, less damaging ways, the spaces were literally stuffed with the work of the executive staff. Quinn Evans/Architects were selected as implementing architects, with the same consultants used elsewhere in the building. Representing Quinn Evans was David Evans, one of the partners, and Stephen Jones, an associate. Nancy Harrison, director of operations for the governor's office, represented Governor Engler in the project. Work went on for more than a year, ending in May 1992. The results were among

The governor's parlor as it appeared originally, around 1879 (bottom). This is matched to the same view after restoration. The parlor under restoration (middle). In the room restored (top), the governor's office and desk can be seen through the inner double doors.

*Top: Photo by Balthazar Korab; middle: photo by Thomas Gennara*
*Bottom left: State Archives of Michigan; bottom right: photo by Balthazar Korab*

the most gratifying in the building, both because of the appeal of the highly developed Victorian character of the rooms and the marked contrast between before and after.

The suite consists of what was originally called the "governor's parlor," the only drawing room in a capitol (the counterpart in most states is the "governor's reception room"); an adjacent office for the governor; and staff offices across the east side of this, on the second floor, and on the main floor. There was space here in which to create a high sense of restoration through furnishing. When the modern partitions were pulled away, the grandeur of the rooms was revealed. The most architecturally interesting was the long one across the east front. Lofty and flooded with light, it gave onto a porch—the one from which Theodore Roosevelt had spoken—of worn sandstone that was magnificent in its sense of age. The view was directly up Michigan Avenue. At one time a reception room, this was made into a secretarial office, divided by a balustrade, with an area in which the governor's callers could wait.

When new, the governor's parlor had been the most popular room in the capitol. The public had flocked here to receptions on New Year's Day and danced in the great halls outside. Any day a citizen could cross the small outer hall and look into the parlor, sometimes seeing the governor at work at his desk, through the double doors.

Somehow this interior, so admired in the nineteenth century, had slipped away. It was the only one of the major spaces in the capitol to have been forgotten. But the Michigan Historical Museum was able to locate many of the elaborate inlaid furnishings from Feige Brothers in Saginaw that had once been in the parlor.

The governor's parlor is the most accurately restored of all the rooms in the capitol. The early photographs which were invaluable in guiding the restoration here do not exist for most rooms in the capitol.
*Photo by Balthazar Korab*

Early photographs as well as drawings in a February 1879 *Harper's Weekly* gave evidence of what the parlor had been like, or at least suggested a tone.

The furniture was collected and, after bidding among qualified competitors, was sent to Brandon Thompson of Alexandria, Virginia, for conservation. After extensive repair its shellac-base french polish was restored. A study of enlargements of old photographs showed that parts of the furniture were missing, for example, the carved spread eagle on the sideboard. All of this was reproduced. A few furnishings of the era supplemented the surviving collection, notably a dining room table and chairs which could serve for conferences. It was determined to use this arrangement, instead of the upholstered furniture in the early pictures, as the governor required that the room double at times for meetings. For the governor's office a new desk was designed in the Victorian manner, a gift to the restoration from the Daughters of the American Revolution, Michigan chapter.

The decorative paint treatments, investigated by Darla Olson, created a triple challenge of conservation, reproduction, and design re-creation. Somehow the ceiling of the parlor had survived, a wondrous Anglo-Japanese fantasy; information could be found to support a reproduction of the wall decorations. However, the decorations of the governor's office were gone. Steve Seebohm of Olson's firm designed an entirely new ceiling for that room, using what survived elsewhere in the suite for inspiration.

Parts of the original glass chandelier of the parlor still exist in private hands, but since they were unavailable and incomplete it was decided to acquire a similar one from the same period. Two were purchased and hung in the parlor and governor's office, and wall brackets of glass and brass were designed to complement them. An upright piano was purchased in place of the lost original. From the old photographs, which were dim and faded, a carpet pattern was devised, following Oriental lines. The sum total, ceiling, carpet, tapestry-covered chairs, the rich and elegant inlay of the historical furniture, all crowned by glass chandeliers, makes a very opulent room, a vignette of a booming Michigan in the days of the timber barons.

In interior work on the office wings carried on by Architects Four for the Senate and by Wigen, Tincknell, Meyer & Associates for the House, the design policies of the master plan for the offices were followed closely. They were to be restored where the facts were known; they were to be modernized only along the original design concepts.

The governor's parlor, from the February 15, 1879, issue of *Harper's Weekly*.

*State Archives of Michigan*

ONLY TWO ROOMS IN THE BUILDING HAVE IDENTICAL COLOR AND DECORATIVE SCHEMES.

Officials agreed that the Capitol Committee held authority over the offices and that they were not to be considered personal spaces. Although adjustments an individual might require would be honored where possible, the decorations and finishing of the offices was to be in step with the overall restoration theme.

Problems came not from within, however, but from without. Beginning in 1989 the Senate and House had purchased antique furniture for the offices, the Senate following its policy that every office have at least one antique piece to enhance the historical idea. The big rooms needed large furniture. Most of what was bought were case pieces, such as cabinets, which had practical use; tables; and in a few instances, chairs. In 1991 the press took hold of the idea as a reflection of political extravagance and elite tastes. What had been spent was quite in step with and often far below the current market costs of comparable new office furniture. But it looked otherwise.

In what was originally the office of the state land commissioners and is now the office of the Speaker of the House, furnishings were designed for modern use while complementing the spacious, high-ceilinged rooms.

*Photo by Dietrich Floeter*

The controversy was typical of the histories of state capitols and echoed the past of this one. Said Jerry Lawler of the Michigan Capitol Committee, "It's not hard for the public to conceive of something that costs millions, like a highway, but a chair or a table costing five hundred bucks—that's another matter." The press coverage ran for some months, but eventually lived out its interest.

The restored offices throughout the capitol would be handsome even considered without their contents, for they are tall and spacious interiors with massive woodwork and heavy doors, and have abundant natural light. Their decorative paint treatments and walnut graining are elegant, and their color schemes incorporate for the most part the earth, sea, leaf, and sky colors known as Pompeiian. Only two rooms in the building have identical color and decorative schemes; details in all are rich and sometimes surprising, varying from Greek key to palm leaves to Japanese motifs of circles and lines. The furniture is for the most part new, much of it made in the skilled hands of the House and Senate carpentry shops.

Some of the furniture was put out to bid, with very particular specifications, and some of the furniture from the carpentry shops was given its surface finish outside the capitol by competitive bid. The furniture is designed for modern purposes but in the old way. Secretaries have credenzas, computer returns, drawers, and work surfaces as convenient as any present-day office furniture, but the look conforms to the period of the capitol. The furniture, together with custom-made carpeting in historic patterns, wooden shutters, lace curtains at some windows, and decorative painting, gives the spaces a cohesiveness known to few offices in any restored public building.

Executive offices are much the same, usually with an antique or two. A comfortable seating area may feature reproduction Victorian overstuffed chairs and a sofa, an antique marble-topped table, and a bookcase salvaged from state library storage. Reproduction clocks equipped with modern movements are available to the offices. Conference rooms have tables copied from surviving tables put in the capitol in the 1870s, designed for Myers's approval by the Strahan Company. They are surrounded today by comfortable "generic" chairs, some of which were also copied from antiques used in the capitol.

Strict rules apply to the hanging of pictures and other items, but it is not prohibited. Capitol staff consult on how this is done, in the interest of protecting the painted walls.

The restoration of the interior ended in the late fall of 1992. In the succession of projects, the capitol's finished glory had been glimpsed only in parts—colorful episodes. The hanging once again of the chandeliers in the great marble-floored corridors seemed the final punctuation. The capitol looked refreshed, returned to what it had been. In a sense it was still what it had always been. The feeling of awe one had always had climbing the grand east stairs to the main level and entering the vast and solemn interior was merely enhanced, not new. It is the work of capitols to stimulate and inspire. Here an early solution to that requirement had been brought again to full life. The job from now on was to keep and maintain, not to rebuild or remodel.

The restoration of the exterior of the capitol began in 1989 and continued until 1992. Time and hard weather had worn the building's face. Its stones had cracked here and there. The massive newel posts on the east stairs were washed nearly to blanks by wind and rain and snow. Water leaked into the walls in places, and the soft brick that backed the stone held it like a sponge. From inside the iron dome one could see outside through little holes like bullet holes, or look at some point where an iron plate had pulled apart from its rivets. Rust had done terrible damage over 114 years.

Restoration of the roof and dome was carried out by Quinn Evans/Architects, represented by David Evans. Consultants included Pat Rice, an expert on cast iron from St. Louis. A new copper roof fulfilled Elijah Myers's and the Michigan legislature's dream of long before (at least in part: the copper was not from Michigan). The dome was surrounded with 100 tons of scaffolding outside, as it was at the same time within, and the iron was carefully cleaned in place, reproduced in parts which had failed because of excessive rust, resealed, primed, and painted by Burdco of Traverse City.

The most visible segment of the restoration: the dome shrouded in scaffolding for repair, stripping, and repainting. Swathing at the colonnade level prevented contamination from old lead-based paint during paint removal.

*Photo by Thomas Gennara*

Exterior stonework, damaged where it had been exposed to salt used in the winter to remove ice from stairs and entrances

*The Christman Company*

Restoration and repair of the interior (left) and exterior (right) of the dome. Rust had taken its toll on lateral I beams, which had to be replaced.

*Photos by Dietrich Floeter*

A worker applies a protective coating to the finial on the lantern above the dome. The tip of the finial is almost 270 feet above the ground.

*Photo by Thomas Gennara*

Exterior metal and stone were cleaned (below) and the stone replaced where necessary, as was the case with column bases on the front steps (bottom).

*Photos by Thomas Gennara*

Work on the dome and sandstone walls took place at approximately the same time, and the roof work followed. Norman Weiss of the conservation program at Columbia University consulted with Steve Jones of Quinn Evans on the stone. Various chemicals were tried but abandoned. At last the solution was reached of using water pressure, and it did the job without doing harm to the stone. Some replacements of stone were necessary and some parts had to be recarved. The exterior work went well, indeed smoothly, until almost the end. It was the matter of a color for the dome. Richard Frank wanted the iron dome painted as Elijah Myers had intended, the color of the sandstone walls, which cleaning had returned to more or less their original color.

There was a public outcry: The dome had always been white!

This was not really the case; its character of seeming to float over the town had been enhanced in the mid-1950s by painting it white and floodlighting it at night. But people considered this by now familiar image a part of their past. Historically the dome had seemed to grow lighter anyway, as nature had aged the stone walls below it to a darker hue than the original stone color. It had never been painted darker to match. The step up to off-white was a natural and simple one, although the white had no connection to the original building. A controversy bubbled in the newspapers, and the Michigan Capitol Committee was flooded with letters. Archivist Kerry Chartkoff patiently told one protester it was necessary that the dome match the stone walls. Undaunted, the protester asked, Why not paint the stone walls to match the dome? Frank's wishes prevailed, although he admits that when he mixed his color he leaned to the light with his "stone" pigment. Everyone was happy.

Worker installing a new copper roof

*Photo by Thomas Gennara*

The Michigan State Capitol, 1992

*Photo by Balthazar Korab*

## Then and Now

That a civilization is largely remembered by what it builds is a well-known fact. Second thought might amend this to say that a civilization is remembered also for what it preserves. One thing is certain: What it tears down is gone forever. Compared to building anew, preservation is a quiet act, but it is a thing of the heart, as well as of the mind and hand, even more than new construction. The Michigan capitol was saved not by architects and builders but by the approval of lawmakers and the people of Michigan. It survived, then, by the same sort of support that saw it built.

The capitol delights us with its Victorian gusto. But it does not belong to one period or to one generation. It belongs to all, those who built it, those who saved it, and those who will keep it. It represents the cumulative history of the people of Michigan. It is their stage for expressing state pride and in its shelter the laws of the state are formed. The citizen finds in the capitol a symbol, visual shorthand for a state government too complex to grasp all at once. In this setting lawmakers take on the credibility of time, for they stand where others have stood and will stand after them. In that sense it is a useful tool, helping and inspiring those who make the laws.

Through the long history of the building, one pauses now and then to remember historic events. It would be difficult here not to recall the generation that built the capitol. The triumph felt by those who won the great war lives on in the building, together with their emotional bond with the Union. Hidden away in Michigan's records is a sermon delivered on Thanksgiving Day 1878, shortly before the capitol was dedicated. The orator was Reverend George Duffield, who told how as a young and lonely chaplain passing through Washington during the Civil War, he had been walking at night down Pennsylvania Avenue and the new dome of the U.S. Capitol, theretofore concealed in clouds, burst suddenly into moonlit view.

"As I approached the Capitol," he said, "it was shrouded in the deepest gloom... Presently there was a rift in the shifting shadows, and I caught sight for the first time of the new dome—in all its towering height, its immense proportions, its sublime magnificence. As I peered curiously through the mist, it seemed... as if in utter defiance of the rebellion and laughing treason to scorn, and daring their united power to do its worst, the mighty symbol of our national authority was steadily advancing to its completion... Then as never before I felt that my first loyalty was to THAT DOME—rather than that of Michigan, Pennsylvania, or any other State—to that dome in the mighty shadow of which all other domes could safely rest."

He and his generation came home from the great conflict to build domes of their own. Imbued with deep feelings of patriotism, and accepting the dome Lincoln had built as the symbol of the Union they had fought to save, they expressed their feelings for their states in monumental architecture of a grandeur that confirmed their own hard-won place in the American nation. Like any eloquent statement born of devotion, this meaning, which permeates the stone, brick, wood, and iron of Michigan's capitol, has remained undiminished through time and as much as anything else assured its restoration.

## AWARDS TO THE MICHIGAN STATE CAPITOL RESTORATION

The restoration of the Michigan State Capitol has received the following architecture, preservation, and restoration awards:

**National Trust 1992 Honor Award**
*National Trust for Historic Preservation*

**1992 AIA Michigan Award of Honor**
*American Institute of Architects Michigan*

**1992 President's Award**
*Michigan Historic Preservation Network*

**Certificate of Recognition**
*American Consulting Engineers Council*

**Honorable Conceptor Award**
*Consulting Engineers Council of Michigan*

**M Award for Excellence in Masonry Design**
*Masonry Institute of Michigan*

**Design and Construction Showcase 1994 Award**
*Construction Association of Michigan;*
*American Institute of Architects, Michigan;*
*Construction Specifications Institute*

**Also:**
*Designated a National Historic Landmark, 1992*

## The Michigan Capitol Committee

Future preservation and maintenance of the Michigan State Capitol are in the hands of the ongoing Michigan Capitol Committee, with offices in Lansing. The committee initiates projects of conservation and restoration of the historic structure and receives gifts of money, historic furnishings, and memorabilia for the capitol.

The Capitol Committee, since its establishment in 1987 through the completion of restoration in 1992 has been composed of the following members:

**1988**

Representative Richard A. Young, *Chair*
Senator William Sederburg, *Vice Chair*
Robert L. Mitchell, *Vice Chair; Deputy Chief Director, Department of Transportation*
Representative Lewis N. Dodak
Representative Michael D. Hayes
Representative James E. O'Neill, Jr.
Senator Dan L. DeGrow
Senator William Faust
Senator John J. H. Schwarz, M.D.
Robert A. Bowman, State Treasurer
Frank J. Kelley, Attorney General
Shelby Solomon, *Director, Department of Management and Budget*

**1989-1990**

Senator William Sederburg, *Chair*
Representative Richard A. Young, *Vice Chair*
Robert L. Mitchell, *Vice Chair; Deputy Chief Director, Department of Transportation*
Representative Pat Gagliardi
Representative Gary L. Randall
Representative James E. O'Neill, Jr.
Senator Dan L. DeGrow
Senator William Faust
Senator John J. H. Schwarz, M.D.
Robert A. Bowman, State Treasurer
William Kandler, *Assistant Chief of Staff and Director of Government Relations, Executive Office*
Shelby Solomon, *Director, Department of Management and Budget*

**1991-1992**

Senator John J. H. Schwarz, M.D.
Jeff McAlvey, *Vice Chair; Legislative Liaison, Executive Office*
Representative Richard A. Young, *Vice Chair*
Senator Dan L. DeGrow
Senator Vernon J. Ehlers
Senator Debbie Stabenow
Representative Pat Gagliardi
Representative Gary L. Randall
Representative James E. O'Neill, Jr.
Colleen Pero, *Director of State Affairs, Executive Office*
Lucille Taylor, *Legal Counsel, Executive Office*

*Michigan Capitol Committee Members, con't.*

**1993-1994**

Lucille Taylor, *Chairman*
*Legal Counsel, Executive Office*
Representative Pat Gagliardi, *Vice Chair*
Representative Gary L. Randall, *Vice Chair*
Senator John J. H. Schwarz, M.D., *Vice Chair*
Jeff McAlvey, *Legislative Liaison,*
*Executive Office*
Sara Saxby, *Administrative Assistant*
*to Deputy Chief of Staff*
John Kost, *Deputy Director,*
*Department of Management and Budget*
Representative Michael J. Bennane
Representative Dan Gustafson
Senator Dan L. DeGrow
Senator Debbie Stabenow
Jerry Lawler, *Executive Director*
Kerry Chartkoff, *Capitol Archivist*

The people of Michigan were invited to the rededication of the Michigan State Capitol, November 19, 1992.

*Photo by David A. Trumpie*